One hundred years of poverty and policy

One hundred years of poverty and policy

**Howard Glennerster, John Hills,
David Piachaud and Jo Webb**

 JOSEPH ROWNTREE
FOUNDATION

The **Joseph Rowntree Foundation** has supported this project as part of its programme of research and innovative development projects, which it hopes will be of value to policy makers, practitioners and service users. The facts presented and views expressed in this report are, however, those of the authors and not necessarily those of the Foundation.

Joseph Rowntree Foundation
The Homestead
40 Water End
York YO30 6WP
Website: www.jrf.org.uk

First published 2004 by the Joseph Rowntree Foundation

ISBN 1 85935 221 9 (paperback)
    1 85935 222 7 (pdf: available at www.jrf.org.uk)

A CIP catalogue record for this report is available from the British Library.

Designed by Adkins Design (www.adkinsdesign.co.uk)
Printed by Fretwells

Further copies of this report, or any other JRF publication, can be obtained either from the JRF website (www.jrf.org.uk/bookshop/) or from our distributor, York Publishing Services, 64 Hallfield Road, York YO31 7ZQ (Tel: 01904 430033).

Photo credits: Pages 16, 17, 30, 66, 72: Mary Evans Picture Library;
20: Museum of London; 45: Joseph Rowntree Foundation; 70: National Archives;
75, 76, 78, 80: Corbis/Hulton-Deutsch Collection; 86: popperfoto.com;
92: Owen Franken/Corbis; 96: Sean Aidan, Eye Ubiquitous/Corbis;
98: Keith Saunders/ArenaPAL.

Cover: Joseph Rowntree Foundation (top), Alamy Images (bottom)

Contents

Figures and tables

Figures

Tables

The Seebohm Rowntree Studentship Fund

Sincere thanks go to the Seebohm Rowntree Studentship Fund for substantial support for the production of this publication. Seebohm Rowntree set aside funds in 1943 to 'help persons who are studying or engaged in research into the causes of poverty and how these can be removed', and 60 years later this charity transferred its remaining assets to the Joseph Rowntree Foundation specifically to support this publication.

The Foundation, and the authors of this volume, pay tribute to the pathbreaking work of Seebohm Rowntree in his study of poverty throughout the first half of the twentieth century. They also place on record their appreciation, to Philip Rowntree, Seebohm Rowntree's son, to Gordon Thorpe, Secretary to the Seebohm Rowntree Studentship Fund for over 40 years, to Andrew Rowntree, Seebohm's grandson, and to Frank Field MP, for their stewardship of this fund.

We are delighted that the name of Seebohm Rowntree can be associated with the publication of this book during the centenary year of his father's creation of what is today the Joseph Rowntree Foundation.

1 Introduction

There is nothing magic about one hundred years that necessarily makes it appropriate as a period over which to review either social policies or their results. Indeed, it is such a long period that it is hard for those looking back with today's concerns and perspectives to understand the contexts within which past policies developed or the ways in which past problems were regarded and understood.

However, for those involved in the study of social problems and policies in the UK, the last century does represent a unique period over which we can think about 'poverty and progress' (or, at times, lack of progress). This is not just because of the centenary of the Joseph Rowntree Foundation's establishment, which this book marks, but because Seebohm Rowntree's study of York in 1899, *Poverty: A study of town life*,[1] gives us the key starting point on which we can peg our understanding of subsequent trends.

It is not our intention to give an evenly paced view of the last century. Rather, it is to look at current concerns taking the longer view of where we have come from – to understand the present, in the light of the past, for the purposes of the future, as John Maynard Keynes put it. In doing this, our perspective, and the structure of the book, are like the famous *New Yorker* cover of a New Yorker's view of the USA, seen from Manhattan – disproportionately dominated by what is nearest, with only a little of what is between the two coasts showing up.

The whole idea of what poverty is and how to measure it has changed a great deal in the past century, although many of the basic issues remain remarkably familiar. We have not attempted to trace this debate in detail, not least because it has been done by others, notably Ruth Lister (2004) in her recent book. However, social scientists' work in measuring and conceptualising poverty has had an impact on policy, and we discuss this at various stages in our account.

In chapter 2, Howard Glennerster sets out the context within which Rowntree carried out his study with the earlier development of empirical investigation by Charles Booth and others, and discusses some of Rowntree's lasting insights.

In chapter 3, David Piachaud and Jo Webb use the evidence from Rowntree's 1899 study of York to try to understand how what we mean by 'poverty' has changed over the last century. What does Rowntree's poverty line mean in today's terms? How do the causes of poverty a century ago compare with its causes today, and what are the key social and economic changes that have led to such differences? In chapter 4 they use evidence not just from Rowntree's three studies of York in 1899, 1936 and 1950, but from a series of other studies both before and after the Second World War, to examine the way in which what was seen as an appropriate 'poverty line' changed over the twentieth century, and what this tells us about the changing extent of poverty over the period.[2]

The second part of the book traces the evolution of policy towards poverty over the century. In chapter 5, Howard Glennerster starts by describing the roots of policy in the poor law tradition, and developments following Rowntree's and Booth's studies. He takes the story from the reforms of Lloyd George, through the post-war reforms associated with (but not always following from) the 1942 Beveridge Report, and the optimism generated by Rowntree's final study to the 'rediscovery of poverty' in the 1960s, and what some have described as the 'end of consensus' in the 1970s.

In chapter 6, John Hills looks at much more recent

developments since inequality and relative poverty started rising in the late 1970s, reviewing policy developments and poverty outcomes under the governments led by Margaret Thatcher, John Major, and Tony Blair.[3]

The last parts of the book look to the future. In chapter 7, John Hills first sets out where Britain now stands in international terms, not just against our own past. While there have been improvements in the most recent period, particularly in respect of child poverty, Britain's position does not compare well with many other countries at a similar level of development. Second, he looks at what constraints and challenges public opinion places on today's policy makers. Third, he looks back a shorter period to the findings of the 1995 Joseph Rowntree Foundation Inquiry into Income and Wealth to see which parts of the agenda set out by the Foundation's Inquiry Group have since been adopted, and which others may still have relevance today. Fourth, he discusses a key part of the context within which future policies will develop – the economic and demographic pressures that will face any British government in the coming decades.

Finally, in chapter 8 we reflect on the policy choices and dilemmas we face today in thinking about policies aimed at reducing poverty and disadvantage, in the light of where we started from a hundred years ago.

Part I
Poverty over the last century

2 The context for Rowntree's contribution

Howard Glennerster

As two American economists have recently shown, the very different approaches societies have taken to fighting poverty lie deep in institutional history, rather than in current economics (Alesina and Glaeser, 2004). This is well illustrated in Britain's distinctive history. The moral and political dilemmas posed by the poor had troubled politicians, social commentators and theologians from the Middle Ages and indeed before. The coming of modern 'political economy' and demography at the end of the eighteenth century, most notably in the writings of Adam Smith and Thomas Malthus, added a tougher and more ruthless logic to the debate. Poverty and starvation might be necessary for population control; 'the scantiness of subsistence can set limits to the further multiplication of the human species,' as Adam Smith put it (1776, p.182).

The need to contain poor relief[1] and how it should be done was a recurrent theme of public debate through the nineteenth century (see chapter 5). By the century's end, however, it was becoming clear to many that the existing order was not able to cope with the demands placed on it by the new international industrial economy in which the United Kingdom played a central part. Many argued that there was a hard core of poverty that was self imposed through wilful indolence and drink. Neither Charles Booth nor Seebohm Rowntree disagreed. But there was also an appreciation that there were growing

Homeless people congregating under a bridge in London, 1870, from the book *London, a Pilgrimage* by Gustav Doré. People both pitied and feared the poor in the mid nineteenth century.

numbers of people whose poverty could not be blamed on individual failings. The prolonged 'unemployment' of the 1880s – a new term at that time (Harris, 1972) – or the Lancashire cotton famine, could not be blamed on a few feckless men and women. Fecklessness hardly went in cycles. The Poor Law was becoming a mainline provider of care to the growing population of elderly women, and of financial support to widows (though eligibility varied widely) and to the sick. It was also a major provider of education and care for poor children.

> *The Poor Law is at the present time only to a small extent concerned with the man who is able-bodied. The various sections of the non-able-bodied – the children, the sick, the mentally defective, and the aged and infirm – make up today nine-tenths of the persons relieved by the Destitution Authorities.*
> (Minority Report of the Royal Commission on the Poor Laws and the Relief of Distress, 1905–9, p. 1)

Appreciating that the old institutions were simply not designed to cope with the new situation took a long time. It was a view vigorously opposed by those in the Local Government Board and the philanthropic Charity Organisation Society whose remedy was to tighten up the way the Poor Law was administered. In 1869 the Poor Law guardians were urged to return to the principles of 1834 and relieve 'able-bodied paupers' only in the workhouse. But the condition of the poor, notably in London, was increasingly becoming both a moral question and a fearful one. The violent demonstrations of the mid 1880s created a fertile ground for descriptions and explanations of what was happening. Poverty in London had been the subject of careful descriptive writing by Henry Mayhew (1861–2) and by others. But it was a powerful pamphlet published by the Congregational Union, *The bitter*

'The crippled street bird-seller', an engraving from Henry Mayhew's influential work *London labour and the London poor* (1861–2). Mayhew's work was one of several bringing the poor to the attention of nineteenth century political thinking.

cry of outcast London: An inquiry into the condition of the abject poor (1883), which sparked widespread attention in the middle class magazines of the time. The working poor were beginning to have their say in an organised way through trade unions. It is at this time that a new social science of poverty measurement begins to play a decisive part in shaping people's understanding and ultimately policy.

Lifting the curtain: The contribution of nineteenth century social science

The *Bitter cry* was an emotional pen portrait. Was it right? Or was it an overblown and unhelpful description that would lead sober reformers in the wrong direction? That is what Charles Booth initially thought.

> *East London lay hidden behind a curtain on which were painted terrible pictures: starving children, suffering women, overworked men; monsters and demons of inhumanity; giants of disease and despair. Did these pictures truly represent what lay behind, or did they bear to the facts a relation similar to that which the pictures outside a booth at some country fair bear to the performance or show within? This curtain we have tried to lift.*
> (Booth, quoted in Abbott, 1917)

His painstaking house by house survey in East London was first reported to meetings of the Royal Statistical Society. It was extended to most of inner London. The accounts of the economic life of each area, the temporary nature of much employment and the low wages even regular employment could generate presented a convincing and much publicised picture. It was not just an attempt to measure the numerical extent of poverty but a mapping of the gradations of human inequality. It was grounded in the local economy of small areas of London. The notion of an inner core of poverty and movements in and out of such areas, which urban sociologists came to refine, are first charted here (Booth, 1888, 1891, 1892–7).

Charles Booth's line of poverty

Booth's most lasting contribution was the means he adopted to provide a definitive answer to the question: were these merely exaggerated journalistic accounts of poverty and distress or were they grounded in solid evidence? In that sense he can be seen as the father of modern poverty study. Booth himself was very sceptical of the claims being made. He changed his mind. The evidence amassed by his investigators convinced him, and his audience at the Royal Statistical Society was not surprised. The survey method he used was by no means modern. He relied on information supplied by and judgements made by local investigators such as the School Board visitors in East London. They went to every family with children of school age. It was assumed that the other half of the working class population was in a similar state. Other volunteers supplemented the work, especially outside the East End. These were not questionnaires filled in or responded to by heads of household. But his assistants were asked to grade their households into what were essentially social groups.

He was not very forthcoming about how he reached the 'line of poverty' used by his investigators.

"By the word poor I mean to describe those who have a fairly regular though bare income, such as 18s to 21s per week for a moderate family, and by 'very poor' those who fall below this standard, whether from chronic irregularity of work, sickness, or a large number of young children."
(Booth's account of his methods given at a meeting of the Royal Statistical Society, May 1887, Journal of the Royal Statistical Society, June 1887; Simey and Simey, 1960, p. 184)

Where on earth did this income level come from? It was much higher than the rates of outdoor relief that the Select

Committee on Poor Relief found in existence in the London of 1888 – an average of 9s 4d (47 new pence) for a family of five. This varied by area and reflected local labour markets. The Poor Law officials asked themselves what was the minimum market wage and how much below it did you need to pay to contain

Part of Charles Booth's 1889 'poverty map' of London. Booth's team of investigators graded each household into social groups, and although the reasoning behind their judgements was not rigorously scientific, the overall pattern of income and poverty showed large areas of chronic need.

the number of paupers? – a test of destitution. What Booth did was to set a rough income level that reflected a judgement about its social acceptability. This was a decisive contribution.

But whose judgement? Recent research suggests it was more firmly grounded than many critics have implied (Gillie, 1996). The source may well have been the fee remission scales used by the London School Board in Tower Hamlets at the time Booth was studying the area. Under the 1870 Education Act it was possible for local boards to make attendance at school compulsory. They were also required to charge fees. That posed difficulties. How far was it reasonable to reduce poor families' incomes? Was there a floor below which it would be irresponsible to do so? Boards in different cities reached their own conclusions about fee remission and kept their yardsticks secret. So did the Tower Hamlets divisional office. But officers had precise guidance about the income at which a prima facie case could be made that it would be socially unacceptable and prejudicial to a child to reduce the family income below that point. Guidance took into account the size of the family and the level of rent paid. It had all the characteristics of modern income support minima and the result was a net income very near to the one Booth chose. He would not have been able to cite this as his source as the Education Board insisted such a scale be kept secret. If this intriguing possibility is correct, the first statistical/social judgement on income adequacy used by Booth may well have been based on a real life judgement by these school board members. But it was not one that could be debated or challenged. This was Seebohm Rowntree's critical contribution.

Rowntree's poverty line

Seebohm's father, Joseph Rowntree, had studied social questions, including 'Pauperism', before Seebohm was born. Seebohm was powerfully affected by a visit to the poorest parts of Newcastle. He discovered Booth's work and wondered if his findings would hold outside London. 'Why not investigate

York?' (Briggs, 1961, p. 17). The methods he used were, at one level, similar to Booth's. House to house visits produced sheets of notes about the accommodation, the numbers in the family and their working occupations and personal remarks about the standard of life, cleanliness and respectability of the inhabitants. The household's broad band of income was mostly estimated from knowledge of the worker's job and the wages paid for that job obtained from the employer. Sometimes the investigator had to rely on the families' own information checked with other observations or a second visit. In addition the investigator was asked to judge from observation, questioning neighbours or members of the family whether, in their view, the family was living in 'obvious want and squalor'. It was this personal judgemental approach that led to the often quoted conclusion that 28 per cent of the total population of York were living in such a state. That compared with the 31 per cent Booth had judged to be in poverty in London. Booth agreed that Rowntree's figures were comparable to his own (Rowntree, 1901; 2001, p. 300).

Whether they really were is a moot point. Helen Bosanquet, of the Charity Organisation Society and member of the Royal Commission on the Poor Laws, questioned why Rowntree's survey of a relatively prosperous market town like York should produce the same result as Booth in the depressed East End of London (Bosanquet, 1903; for an account of contemporary critics see Bowpitt, 2000).

What was new, and was to have a long term impact on poverty measurement, was his attempt to measure the causes of poverty. Rowntree distinguished those whose income was so low that even if they followed complete sobriety and total purchasing efficiency they would not be able to live at a level of 'physical efficiency'.

His attempts here have often been misunderstood. He knew that any figure was likely to be attacked, as it was to be by the Charity Organisation Society and others. So he sought a harder, he hoped unchallengeable, measure. The adviser he turned to was an American who was working for the US Department of Agriculture, Professor W. O. Atwater, whose specialist area was human nutrition and energy, backed up by two nutritionists from Scotland. How much food of what kind did a working man need to function as an effective worker? That depended on the type of work he was doing, Atwater argued, and he produced a range of minimum diets from that needed by workers who used little physical exercise, through moderate to active muscular work. The moderate standard was chosen.

Then Rowntree switched to actual food budgets. Here he took the rations set out by the Local Government Board recommended for those in workhouses, and the cheapest one at that. They seemed to produce a diet consistent with the nutritional level proposed by Atwater for men. The rations for women and children could be roughly adopted and turned into a household budget by using prices available to the working class in York and checked against actual working class diets in York and those of American workers. He concluded that 'the labouring classes on whom the bulk of the muscular work falls, are seriously underfed' (1901, p. 259).

What Rowntree was doing was essentially to throw down the gauntlet and challenge his critics: 'Are you seriously suggesting that you can expect families to live on less than this?' It was this harsher, apparently more 'scientific', measure he called 'primary poverty'.

The difference between the judgemental levels of 'squalid living' and his primary poverty level formed the controversial gap he called 'secondary poverty'. These were 'families whose total earnings would be sufficient for the maintenance of merely physical efficiency *were it not that some portion of it is absorbed by other expenditure, either useful or wasteful*' (1901, p. 115; emphasis in the original). Only 10 per cent of the York population were living in primary poverty, or 15 per cent of the wage earning class.

The physical efficiency claim that underpinned the primary poverty idea had an immediate appeal because of the growing

> ## Box 1 **The life cycle of poverty**
>
> Rowntree described a life cycle of poverty as follows:
>
> *The life of a labourer is marked by five alternating periods of want and comparative plenty. During early childhood, unless his father is a skilled worker, he probably will be in poverty; this will last until he, or some of his brothers or sisters, begin to earn money and thus augment their father's wage sufficiently to raise the family above the poverty line. Then follows the period during which he is earning money and living under his parent's roof; for some portion of this period he will be earning more money than is required for lodging, food, and clothes. This is his chance to save money. If he has saved enough to pay for furnishing a cottage, this period of comparative prosperity may continue after marriage until he has two or three children, when poverty will again overtake him. This period of poverty will last perhaps for ten years, i.e. until the first child is fourteen years old and begins to earn wages; but if there are more than three children it may last longer. While the children are earning, and before they leave home to marry, the man enjoys another period of prosperity – possibly, however, only to sink back again into poverty when his children have married and left him, and he himself is too old to work, for his income has never permitted his saving enough for him and his wife to live upon for more than a very short time.*
>
> *A labourer is thus in poverty, and therefore underfed –*
>
> *(a) In childhood – when his constitution is being built up.*
> *(b) In early middle life – when he should be in his prime.*
> *(c) In old age.*

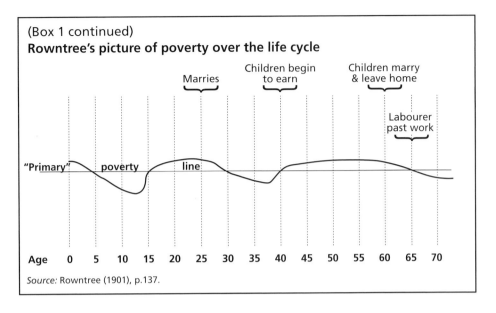

(Box 1 continued)

Rowntree's picture of poverty over the life cycle

Source: Rowntree (1901), p.137.

debate in the late 1890s about 'national efficiency'. Those on such wages could not be fully productive workers was the implication. Veit-Wilson (1986) argues that it is the visible life style of want and squalor that was really at the centre of Rowntree's moral concern. No one could really be expected to live on his primary poverty income in real social life. Social pressures, to drink in the local pub, to buy presents for the children, to be a normal social being especially in adversity, required a higher budget. This was the burden of Townsend's later critique (1954, 1962, 1979).

That may be so, but what gave Rowntree his supposed authority was the emphasis he placed on diet and household budgets, which take up much of the book and its appendices. It was this idea that appealed to later investigators, as Veit-Wilson (1994) points out, and they made studies of other English cities, to be discussed in the next chapter.

Rowntree himself developed a more generous measure in his 'human needs of labour' study (1918), as we shall see. And by the time of his second survey of York in 1936 (Rowntree, 1941), Rowntree had abandoned the idea of secondary poverty:

In this survey I have made no attempt to measure the

amount of 'secondary' poverty by direct observation, partly because the methods of doing this adopted in 1899 appear to me now as being too rough to give reliable results, and also because even had I done so the results would not have rendered possible a comparison with 1899 for ideas of what constitutes 'obvious want and squalor' have changed profoundly since then ... the only figures that are absolutely comparable are those for primary poverty.
(1941, p. 461)

Whatever Rowntree's original intentions then, the idea of poverty measures based on diet and physical efficiency had taken on a life of its own.

A crucial insight: The life cycle of poverty

What was equally important for future poverty study was Rowntree's attempt to unravel the causes of poverty. He demonstrated that the rewards the labour market generated in *normal* times were ill adapted to meet the basic needs of family life for many of the working population, notably during childrearing and widowhood, sickness and old age. Observing from his returns the circumstances of families in poverty he formulated his life cycle of poverty theory, going on to elaborate it later in the *The human needs of labour* (Rowntree, 1918) (see box 1, pages 24–25).

Wages, he argued, derived from the interaction of supply and demand for particular skills. There was no reason why they should take account of the fluctuating income needs of families over their life cycle especially the coming of children or the varying size of family. The significant activity of friendly societies, Rowntree noted, helped to explain the low level of primary poverty experienced from sickness and old age. The economy was prospering at the top of the economic cycle. The level of wages relative to the needs of a family with several children was simply too low to meet the most basic nutritional needs of many families.

Women's contribution

The attention Booth and Rowntree's work has attracted has
tended to obscure important research done at the time by
women's groups, such as the Fabian Women's Group and others
who were involved in the Suffragette Movement. Much of their
work was qualitative and it explored the meaning and
experience of poverty for individual family members and
notably women. It was influential because it gave an accessible
parallel account to that of Rowntree. It provided accounts of
the way in which women struggled to cope on below poverty
wages. It also raised issues about the distribution of income
within families that feminists were to rediscover in the 1980s.

An example was Mrs Pember Reeves' (1914) Fabian
pamphlet, *Family Life on a Pound a Week*. It set out to answer
the question 'How does a Lambeth working man's wife with
four children manage on a pound a week?' The answer differed
not least because the dietary (and other!) demands of men
varied and what was left determined what was available for
the children's and the wife's needs. This was the era of the male
breadwinner family but many women were also single and had
family responsibilities of various kinds – more, these studies
found, than Rowntree had claimed. It was an era of significant
widowhood. Poverty has not *become* feminised – it always was
(Lewis and Piachaud, 1992).

In short, new social science evidence was posing an alternative to
the traditional view of poverty that it was the result of personal
failing and could be countered only by personal change which
required the absence of easy state poor relief. Explanations we
are familiar with today – unemployment generated by economic
cycles, the changing needs of families over their life cycle and the
rigidity of wages compared to changing family needs over a life
time – were already formulated. So, too, were the distinctive
needs of the sick, the old and those with long term disabilities
who could not be blamed for their situation. Social scientists and
actuarial statisticians were coming to see that individuals and

families faced a range of economy-wide risks that it was very difficult for them to insure against privately or collectively in work-based or local self help societies. Some kinds of employment or even location made the risks of ill health difficult to insure against in small local or occupation-based organisations. One way to see the history of the next half century is the dawning realisation that there were fundamental market and self help failures that required some kind of state action to correct the causes of poverty. Incomes were too low and insecure for many to save enough for their own retirement. Those most prone to ill health were least likely to be able to sustain sick clubs or private insurance without support. The 'risk pool' had to be widened if families' risks of poverty were to be minimised (Johnson, 1996). Economy-wide solutions had to be found for unemployment. Moreover, the scale and depth of each of these groups' risks were to change through the coming century. Increasingly the politics of the twentieth century would become concerned with the question – who should pay the costs of sharing such risks (Baldwin, 1990)? Should it be the whole community, the rich or only the working class? We trace threads of that story in part 2.

In the following chapters, however, we look at how Seebohm Rowntree's legacy of local poverty studies was continued up to the Second World War and how the scale of poverty on different measures changed over the century. We use the analysis of the causes of poverty pioneered by Seebohm Rowntree to examine how far those causes changed.

3 Changes in poverty

David Piachaud and Jo Webb

Rowntree's 1899 study provides a baseline for considering how poverty has changed over the twentieth century. This chapter reviews the main studies of poverty published in the twentieth century and compares Rowntree's first study based on his survey of York in 1899 with evidence about poverty in Britain at the start of the twenty-first century. In the next section these studies are described and then the chapter examines how the poverty lines or standards used in these studies compare and how the extent of poverty has changed. In the next chapter the changing causes of poverty are analysed. Examining changes in poverty is purely descriptive and historical unless it illuminates understanding of why changes occurred: some the main social and economic changes that occurred over the century are considered and their impact on poverty is discussed.

Poverty studies

Seebohm Rowntree's *Poverty: A study of town life* was based on York, the home of Rowntree and his family's chocolate factory. He wrote that 'My object in undertaking the investigation . . . was, if possible, to throw some light upon the conditions which govern the life of the wage-earning classes in provincial towns, and especially upon the problem of poverty' (1901, p. vii). Rowntree is best remembered for developing and formalising the concept of the poverty line, collecting details about the income of each household, rather than just making rough guesses, making a distinction between what he called 'primary' and 'secondary' poverty, and the concept of poverty over the life cycle, as discussed in chapter 2.

Subsequently other investigators followed in Rowntree's footsteps. In 1903 a survey which seems largely to have been forgotten was carried out by Mann (1905). It is interesting since it looked at a rural area, a village in Bedfordshire, whereas almost all the other early surveys looked at towns.

The next landmark in poverty studies was provided by Bowley and Burnett-Hurst (1915, 1920), published under the title *Livelihood and poverty*. The study covered five towns (Reading, Northampton, Warrington, Stanley and Bolton) and was carried out between 1912 and 1914. They followed Rowntree's broad approach but Bowley, a trained statistician at the London School of Economics, pioneered the use of random sampling, with far-reaching consequences. Abrams observed that surveys 'were no longer dependent on the munificence of millionaire philanthropists and upon the years of toil of wealthy amateurs' (1951, p. 44). A follow-up to *Livelihood and*

A dole queue in 1911. As political concern about poverty increased, social security was gradually extended, but was still often subject to stringent means tests.

poverty carried out by Bowley and Hogg in 1923–4, published under the title *Has poverty diminished?* (1925), dealt with a subject of great contemporary interest, the difference between the prewar and the post-war world.

The biggest survey in the interwar period was the New Survey of London Life and Labour directed by Hubert Llewellyn-Smith (1930–5), which specifically aimed to provide a comparison with Booth's earlier study.

There was a flurry of surveys in the 1930s, including surveys of Sheffield (Owen, 1933), Merseyside (Jones, 1934), Southampton (Ford, 1934), Plymouth (Taylor, 1938), and a survey of Bristol (Tout, 1938), which was technically interesting as probably the first in Britain to use the Hollerith punch-card machine (Wardley and Woollard, 1994).

Rowntree's second survey of York, published as *Poverty and progress* (1941), was particularly interesting since it showed how much social conditions had changed between 1899 and 1936. Rowntree measured poverty according to several different standards, the original 1899 level and a rather more generous line based on his study of the *Human needs of labour* (1937) – so this study looked forward as well as back. His third survey in 1950, much smaller and less rigorous than his earlier studies, found that poverty had been virtually abolished largely as a result of the welfare state, an apparent achievement of the Beveridge reforms which was widely reported. This was the last of the old style local poverty surveys.

The introduction of the official Family Expenditure Survey (FES) was a watershed for poverty research. This was carried out on a one-off basis in 1953/54 and then on a continuous basis from 1957 onwards. Its primary purpose is to collect information about expenditure patterns which is used to construct the Retail Price Index, but it also collected information about household incomes. Initially this information was fairly crude, but the questions became more detailed over time. FES data could therefore be used to look at poverty at a national level. The first to recognise and seize this opportunity were a group of academics based at the London School of Economics. In the early 1960s Peter Townsend (1962) and Dorothy Wedderburn (1962) presented some preliminary results from an analysis of the FES for the years 1953/54 and 1960. The final results were published with much publicity, and the linked establishment of the Child Poverty Action Group, in December 1965 in a pamphlet by Abel-Smith and Townsend, called *The poor and the poorest.*

Many further analyses were conducted in the same mould using the FES in the 1960s and 1970s, including those by Atkinson (1969), Fiegehen, Lansley and Smith (1977) and Beckerman and Clark (1982).

Official statistics on low incomes became a regular series with the publication of the *Low Income Families* estimates between 1972 and 1985 (DHSS, 1988). These were based on the FES and the format of the analyses was very similar to those produced by Abel-Smith and Townsend, although the word 'poverty' was not mentioned.

The current official statistics on low incomes can be found in the annual *Households Below Average Income* (HBAI) report, which began to be published in 1988 and replaced the official Low Income Families series. Originally this used the FES but it is now based on the larger, tailor-made Family Resources Survey carried out on behalf of the Department for Work and Pensions. As its name suggests, HBAI provides details about various aspects of the lower half of the income distribution, but many commentators have chosen 50 per cent of mean income or 60 per cent of median income, as a convenient poverty line. In 1999 this appeared to receive official endorsement in the form of a set of poverty indicators published by the government (DSS, 1999) and was used in the Public Service Agreement target for cutting child poverty by one quarter by 2004/05. The latest target in the *Child poverty review* (HM Treasury, 2004) is to halve child poverty defined as below 60 per cent of median income level (before housing costs) by 2010/11 relative to the 1998/99 level.

Poverty lines

There are many differences in the poverty studies mentioned here: in who carried out and financed the surveys, the population covered, sampling and survey size, sources of information and their quality, response rates, and representativeness.[1] Most fundamental in describing poverty is what is meant by 'poverty' – what line or standard was used. The starting point is Rowntree.

Rowntree drew up his 'primary' poverty line, as described in chapter 2, based in part on science and in part on observation. The scientific input was from American nutritionists whose research (however unethical in retrospect, being based on involuntary convict subjects) indicated requirements for 'the maintenance of merely physical efficiency'. To this was added the cost of clothing, light and fuel.

On rents, Rowntree wrote:

In estimating the necessary minimum expenditure for rent, I should have preferred to take some reliable standard of accommodation required to maintain families of different sizes in health, and then to take as the minimum expenditure the average cost in York of such accommodation. This course would, however, have assumed that every family could obtain the needful minimum accommodation, which is far from being the case.

In view, therefore, of the difficulty of forming an estimate as above, the actual sums paid for rent have been taken as the necessary minimum rent expenditure. *Extravagance in this item is very improbable, rent being the first thing in which a poor family will try to economise.*
(1901, p. 106, emphasis in original)

This issue is still with us – exemplified by the continuing struggles of the government to reform Housing Benefit. Most subsequent studies of poverty have either included actual rents in setting the poverty line or, with the same effect, studied incomes after housing costs. For comparability, the same will be done here.

The table below shows the minimum necessary expenditures per week in 1899.[2]

	Food	Sundries	Total
Each adult	3s	2s 6d	5s 6d
Each child	2s 3d	7d	2s 10d

The diet this allowed was bleak indeed. It is set out in box 2.

Box 2 Rowntree's 1899 diet

For a man Rowntree's 1899 diet comprised the following (the days from Wednesday to Saturday were no different):

	Breakfast	Dinner	Supper
Sunday	Bread, 8 oz Margarine, ½ oz Tea, 1 pt	Boiled bacon, 3 oz Pease pudding, 12 oz	Bread, 8 oz Margarine, ½ oz Cocoa, 1 pt
Monday	Bread, 8 oz Porridge, 1½ pts	Potatoes with milk, 24 oz Bread, 2 oz Cheese, 2 oz	Bread, 8 oz Vegetable broth, 1 pt Cheese, 2 oz
Tuesday	Porridge, 1½ pts Skim milk, 1 pt	Vegetable broth, 1 pt Bread, 4 oz Cheese, 2 oz Dumpling, 8 oz	Bread, 4 oz Porridge, 1½ pts

---

(Box 2 continued)

The table below compares the prices of food items in 1899 and 2004, expressed in current prices converted to (new) pence per pound (2004 prices are April 2004 Waitrose prices, London).

	1899	2004	Increase
Flour	0.48	15	31x
Oatmeal	0.83	34	41x
Cheese	2.71	212	78x
Sugar	0.73	31	42x
Potatoes	0.21	18	86x
Margarine	3.33	47	14x
Butter	5.0	141	28x
Biscuits	1.67	44	27x
Bacon	5.0	135	27x
Tea	7.08	307	43x
Coffee	5.0	899	180x
Treacle	0.73	79	108x
Onions	0.21	25	119x
Currants	1.46	97	67x
Milk (per pint)	0.63	30	48x

The cost of some components of the diet then and now are also shown in the box. Costing the weekly diet for a man and for children aged 3–8 at today's prices gives totals of £10.70 and £5.60 per week respectively. The cost of the diet made up over half of the total poverty line for adults and four-fifths of the total for children.

Comparisons between the poverty lines used in other studies are fraught with difficulty, due to differences in their structures and lack of suitable price indices and measures of living standards. The poverty lines used in the early studies are as consistently as possible compared in figure 1; this relates to a three-child family and is adjusted to the price levels of 2000. It is clear that most of the early surveys used similar poverty lines

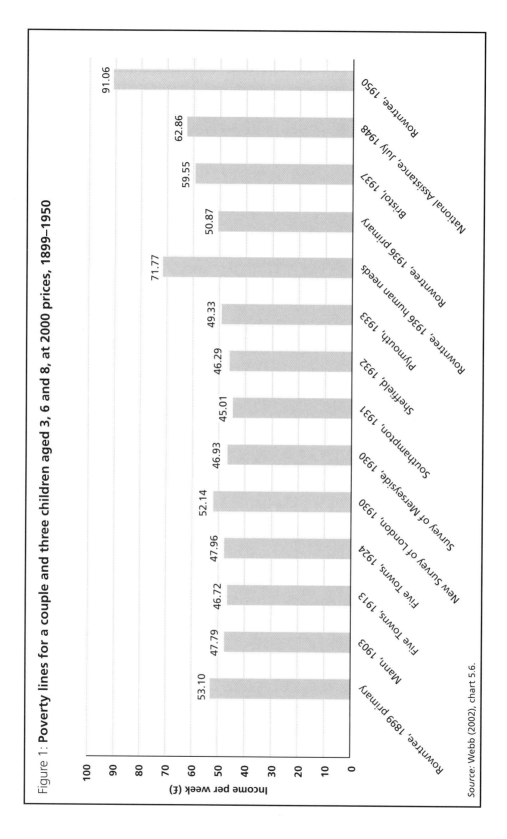

Figure 1: **Poverty lines for a couple and three children aged 3, 6 and 8, at 2000 prices, 1899–1950**

Study	Income per week (£)
Rowntree, 1899 primary	53.10
Mann, 1903	47.79
Five Towns, 1913	46.72
Five Towns, 1924	47.96
New Survey of London, 1930	52.14
Survey of Merseyside, 1930	46.93
Southampton, 1931	45.01
Sheffield, 1932	46.29
Plymouth, 1933	49.33
Rowntree, 1936 human needs	71.77
Rowntree, 1936 primary	50.87
Bristol, 1937	59.55
National Assistance, July 1948	62.86
Rowntree, 1950	91.06

Source: Webb (2002), chart 5.6.

in real terms and in structure. By the 1930s these lines were very low in comparison with general living standards. The main exception was Rowntree, who in his second and third studies was much more generous than the rest.

In the second half of the century, benefit levels did not change their structure much until very recently, with higher allowances for children, especially younger ones. Means tested social assistance benefits increased roughly in line with average incomes until the early 1980s, and have risen sporadically since then, as shown in figure 2.

Overall, the derivation of poverty lines and the fine details of their construction, such as the varying treatment of men, women, pensioners, children and people of working age, have changed over time, but the measures produced have been surprisingly stable when viewed in relation to living standards. In the first half of the century, poverty lines for a single man were 30–35 per cent of weekly personal disposable income per capita, while in the second half they were around 40 per cent, as shown in figure 3 (page 40). For a three-child family there was much more variation from about 80 to 140 percent of per capita income.

We can compare Rowntree's 1899 primary poverty level with the equivalised 60 per cent of median income standard now used by the government. The overall poverty levels have been expressed as proportions of consumers' expenditure per capita, as shown in table 1. It can be seen that for all types of household the poverty line has not only increased with rising prosperity but has risen somewhat relative to average expenditure levels. (It may be noted that the poverty line for 2001/02 is considerably higher than Income Support levels, which are roughly similar proportions of average consumption per head as were Rowntree's primary poverty levels.)

At the end of the twentieth century, poverty lines were far higher in absolute (real) terms than ever before, but in relative terms they had changed rather little. All the evidence suggests that over a long period of time, the public has regarded the

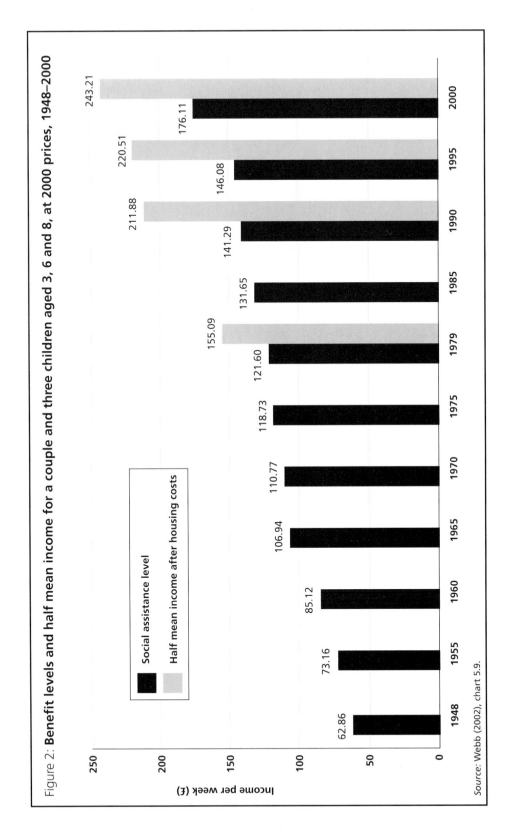

Figure 2: **Benefit levels and half mean income for a couple and three children aged 3, 6 and 8, at 2000 prices, 1948–2000**

Source: Webb (2002), chart 5.9.

Table 1: **Poverty lines as a proportion of consumers' expenditure per capita (%)**

	Single person	Couple, no children	Couple, one child (8–10)	Couple, two children	Couple, three children	Single person, one child
1899	36	60	78	97	114	55
2001/02	42	76	93	111	128	59

Source: Piachaud (1988) for Rowntree's 1899 'primary poverty' line; authors' calculations for 2001/02.

poverty line as a relative concept, i.e. bearing some relation to general living standards although not necessarily rising quite as fast as they do. Although social policy textbooks often talk about 'absolute' versus 'relative' definitions of poverty, and the person usually cited as an exponent of the former view is Rowntree, this is a gross misrepresentation of his work. Budget standards became stuck in a rut in the 1930s because researchers were concentrating on making comparisons, either with different places or different times, not because they were seen as currently valid. Surveys of public opinion indicate that over time, people's views of necessities and the income required to afford them do rise upwards as average incomes grow.[3] As Donnison said in 1982:

> *Supplementary benefit today is worth about twice as much as national assistance was as recently as 1948. So why worry about the poor? Poverty means exclusion from the living standards, the life styles and the fellowship of one's fellow citizens. That exclusion is not experienced merely as a frustrating failure to keep up with the Joneses. The assistant secretary in charge of the campaign against fraud who believed that everyone could manage perfectly well with an income equivalent to the national assistance rates of his boyhood on which his own parents lived had forgotten that they had an open fire and probably a cooking range which*

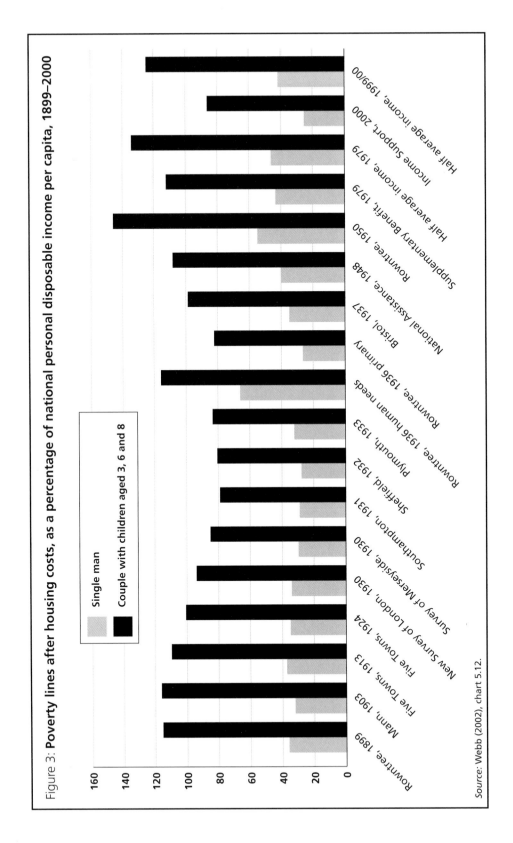

Figure 3: **Poverty lines after housing costs, as a percentage of national personal disposable income per capita, 1899–2000**

Legend:
Single man
Couple with children aged 3, 6 and 8

Categories:
Rowntree, 1899
Mann, 1903
Five Towns, 1913
Five Towns, 1924
New Survey of London, 1930
Survey of Merseyside, 1930
Southampton, 1931
Sheffield, 1932
Plymouth, 1933
Rowntree, 1936 human needs
Rowntree, 1936 primary
Bristol, 1937
National Assistance, 1948
Rowntree, 1950
Supplementary Benefit, 1979
Half average income, 1979
Income Support, 2000
Half average income, 1999/00

Source: Webb (2002), chart 5.12.

could burn all kinds of fuel. They were not compelled to live in a flat with one of the more expensive forms of central heating. They could probably grow vegetables in the back garden, and walk to the shops every day – little shops which would give you credit if you were short of cash. They had no need of a refrigerator for storing their food. They could hang out the washing in the yard and had no need of launderettes or washing machines. Since no-one had television sets their children would not have felt at a loss in the playground and the classroom for lack of what has now become most people's main window on the world – almost the only window for those who cannot afford to go anywhere.
(1982, p. 226)

Contemporary examples are the reduction in public telephone booths due to the prevalence of mobile phones, and the much wider range of information and services available to those with internet access.

The current poverty line based on a proportion of average income is convenient to apply – particularly when making international comparisons – and easy to understand, but its apparent simplicity disguises a host of technical definitions and implicit assumptions. It is possible to imagine a very rich society where nobody lacked what people in any other society would see as necessities and yet some people still had incomes below half average.

The modern approach to defining needs that is closest to Rowntree's method is the Budget Standard approach, expounded most notably by Jonathan Bradshaw (1993). This approach was for a long time associated with discredited notions of 'absolute' poverty. But there is nothing intrinsically absolute or fixed about it, although it is rather laborious to update. It has the great advantage that it is explicit, and there is no reason why the 'necessities' included should not change over time.[4]

Budget standards incorporating public opinion could be used to supplement the 60 per cent of median income measure to counteract the criticism that it is arbitrary and abstract. Such standards have been constructed recently for several family types, giving a detailed picture of what different households need to achieve a particular standard of living in the UK at a specific point in time. Far from Rowntree's diet of cocoa, pease pudding and boiled bacon, they take into account items necessary for modern families, including childcare costs, which made a big difference to the picture. These budgets have been constructed after wide consultation with relevant groups, not just by 'experts'.

It is striking that at the end of the twentieth century, budget standards and 60 per cent of median income were producing quite similar results despite being constructed in completely different ways. The two approaches complement each other well. One strategy would be that from time to time, budget standards could be compared with average income to determine what proportion of average income should be used as the poverty line – a proportion that might gradually change as time went on. The HBAI report could also discuss how the poverty line translates in terms of living standards – a way of putting flesh on the bones of the statistical calculations to make them more meaningful.

A problem which has been exacerbated in recent years is the divergence between the poverty measure in common use and the social security system. Some discrepancies may be justified: for example, the benefit system uses the 'inner family' unit as the benefit unit, whereas the HBAI series is based on households. For the purposes of poverty measurement it is probably fair to assume that most individuals in a household share resources with each other, while for the benefit system to make this assumption would be politically unacceptable. But there is little rationale for other inconsistencies: 60 per cent of median income is now considerably higher than benefit level for most family types; clearly there is a serious gap between what society and the government regard as an appropriate poverty line and the standard of living it is prepared to grant in practice to people receiving benefits.

The changing extent of poverty

Rowntree's study was confined to York. As Rowntree himself put it: 'One naturally asks on reading these figures [on poverty in York] how far they represent the proportion of poverty in other towns' (1901, p. 298). He described York as 'this typical provincial town' (p. 304) and before undertaking his study he satisfied himself 'that the conditions of life obtaining in my native city of York were not exceptional, and that they might be taken as representative of the condition existing in many, if not most, of our provincial towns'. Comparing his results with Booth's earlier study of London, Rowntree wrote: 'The proportion of the population living in poverty in York may be regarded as practically the same as in London' (p. 299).

Jonathan Bradshaw in his preface to the centennial edition of Rowntree's study wrote:

> *We concluded that Rowntree's claim that conditions of life in York were not exceptional and were fairly representative is remarkably true of the city a century later (with reservations on ethnic mix). In terms of the key determinants of living standards, including rates of pay, levels of unemployment, proportion of the population who are sick or disabled, lone-parent families, retirement pensioners or people who are in receipt of income-related benefits, York is extraordinarily close to the national average.*
> (Rowntree, 2000, pp. lxv–lxvi)

Thus it seems justifiable to treat Rowntree's study as broadly representative of Britain and to compare poverty in York in 1899 with that in Britain at the end of the century – besides which, we have no choice.

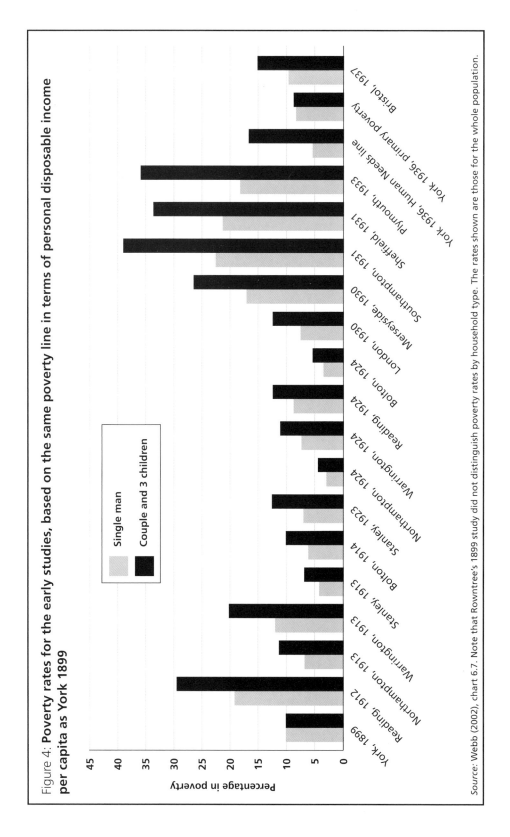

Figure 4: **Poverty rates for the early studies, based on the same poverty line in terms of personal disposable income per capita as York 1899**

Source: Webb (2002), chart 6.7. Note that Rowntree's 1899 study did not distinguish poverty rates by household type. The rates shown are those for the whole population.

Slums in York, a 'typical provincial town', circa 1900. Seebohm Rowntree's influential work, *Poverty: A study of town life* (1901), measured, among other things, the cost of 'mere physical subsistence'. He produced measures of numbers in primary poverty (below this level) and in secondary poverty (above this level but living in 'squalor'), attempting to take a more scientific approach to the study of poverty.

Rowntree found that 9.9 per cent of York's population were below his primary poverty line, or living in 'primary poverty'. In addition nearly twice this proportion – 17.9 per cent – were living above the poverty line but in 'obvious want and squalor', which is Rowntree's 'secondary poverty'. Together this made a total of 27.8 per cent living in poverty.

The extent of poverty found in subsequent studies up to 1937 is shown in figure 4, but with results adjusted to use the same *relative* standard as the 'primary poverty' line in Rowntree's 1899 study. The broad picture is one of some decline comparing the 1920s with the years before the First World War, and higher rates of poverty in the early 1930s than in the 1920s.

Poverty in 1950 was underestimated by Rowntree, and it increased during the 1950s, as Abel-Smith and Townsend showed. Even then, it was at very low levels by modern standards, affecting less than 4 per cent of the population if the standard benefit level was used as the poverty line. Abel-Smith and Townsend's 'rediscovery' of poverty was in part due to the

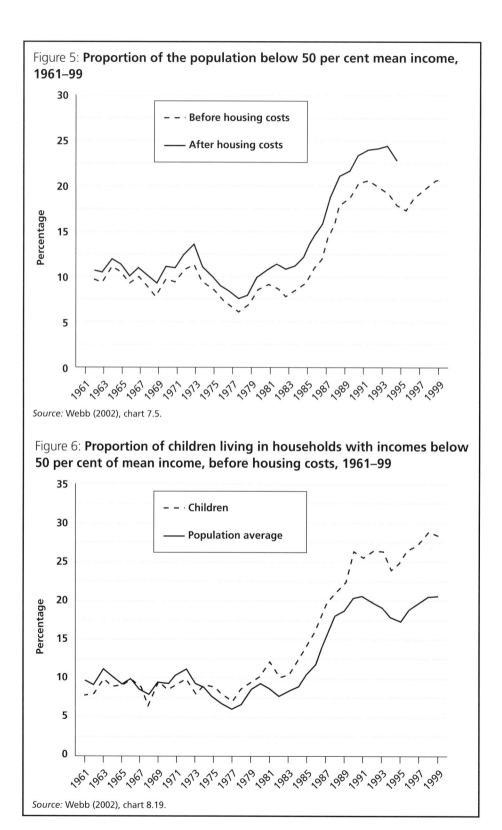

Figure 5: **Proportion of the population below 50 per cent mean income, 1961–99**

Legend:
- - - Before housing costs
——— After housing costs

Source: Webb (2002), chart 7.5.

Figure 6: **Proportion of children living in households with incomes below 50 per cent of mean income, before housing costs, 1961–99**

Legend:
- - - Children
——— Population average

Source: Webb (2002), chart 8.19.

use of a higher poverty line, 140 per cent of the basic 'scale rates' of benefit (on the basis that this allowed for other 'extras' people on National Assistance could get on top of scale rates), which produced a poverty rate of 14.2 per cent.

The 1960s and 1970s were a period of relative stability, with poverty still in single figures on the standard benefit level measure, and only around 10 per cent on a half mean income measure. The extent of post-war poverty over the period for which continuous data are available is shown in figure 5. The great change came in the 1980s, when it doubled to roughly 20 per cent, and stayed there until the end of the century. The period since the late 1970s is considered in more detail in chapter 6.

Among children, the extent of poverty, as measured by their family income level, was close to the average of all ages until the 1980s. Since then child poverty has become markedly more severe, as shown in figure 6.

In 2001/02, over one person in five (22 per cent) was living below the poverty line of 60 per cent of median income level (after housing costs). No attempt had been made since Rowntree's first study to measure secondary poverty since doing so involved a highly subjective judgement on the part of the researcher. This in part reflected the quest for objectivity in poverty research but also the primacy given in twentieth century social science to the quantitative over the qualitative.

Having considered the poverty lines used and the overall extent of poverty in twentieth century Britain, it is to the changing pattern and causes of poverty that the next chapter turns.

4 Why has poverty changed?

David Piachaud and Jo Webb

Causes of poverty

Rowntree distinguished six causes of poverty and divided those in primary poverty according to these causes. The division is shown in table 2. Over half the poor were in regular work but at low wages.

To examine how far Rowntree's 'causes' continue to explain poverty, data from the Family Resources Survey for 2001/02[1] have been reanalysed using as far as possible the same categories as Rowntree.[2] The results in table 2 show important changes.

The biggest group in poverty remains households with someone in work, but these account for only one third of those now in poverty. Largeness of families (five or more children) has greatly declined in significance from 22 to 2 per cent. Illness or old age of the chief wage earner has grown in importance but widowhood is less significant. Unemployment is now more important than a century ago in explaining poverty. There is now a large group whose poverty is not explained by any of Rowntree's causes; these include lone parent families, students and others.

Counting how many fall below a poverty line gives a measure of poverty but it does nothing to indicate the severity of poverty; in a head count those a few pence below the poverty line count equally with those far below the level. To indicate severity it is possible to derive 'poverty gaps' which measure the deficit below the poverty line. Rowntree

Table 2: **Causes of poverty, 1899 and 2001/02**

| | Make-up of poor (%) | | Proportion poor (%) |
	1899 (primary poverty)	2001/02 (below 60% of median)	2001/02
Death of chief wage earner	15.6	5.8	23.7
Illness or old age of chief wage earner	5.1	25.7	30.1
Chief wage earner out of work/ unemployed	2.3	8.6	73.0
Largeness of family	22.2	2.1	65.0
Irregularity of work	2.8	} 31.0	} 11.1
In regular work but at low wage	52.0		
Other	–	26.8	52.5
All causes	100.0	100.0	22.0

Source: Rowntree (1901), p.120; authors' calculations using Family Resources Survey, 2001/02, see notes 1 and 2 to this chapter.

calculated these for each of his main categories of the poor. As far as possible this has been reproduced for 2001/02. The results are shown in table 3. In both years, the group falling farthest below the poverty level was those in unemployed households, still with an income less than half of the current poverty line. The relative severity of poverty in households with one or more in regular work was greater in 2001/02 than 1899. For widows not only the incidence but also the severity of poverty had diminished.

Taking the century as a whole, some conclusions can be drawn about the composition of the poor and the causes of poverty. Although surveys used different methods and poverty lines, at any given time there was general agreement about the leading cause. The earliest studies found that poverty was mainly due to the combination of low wages and large families, and child poverty rates were very high. In the 1920s and 1930s, unemployment became a huge problem, and the unemployed had a high risk of falling into poverty, despite unemployment

Table 3: **Poverty gaps as a percentage of the poverty line**

	1899	2001/02
Death of chief wage earner	} 36.9	25.2
Illness or old age of chief wage earner		26.6
Chief wage earner out of work/unemployed	83.6	51.6
Largeness of family	10.0	19.0
Irregularity of work	31.1	} 41.1
In regular work but at low wages	24.8	

Source: Rowntree (1901), p.120; authors' calculations using Family Resources Survey, 2001/02, see notes 1 and 2 to this chapter.

insurance and assistance. After the war, family allowances eased the problem of low wages, and unemployment was very low. The largest group in poverty in the 1950s and 1960s were the elderly, many of whom did not claim the National Assistance to which they were entitled. When poverty was 'rediscovered' in the 1960s, public attention was drawn to the plight of children in poverty. Pensioners were still more likely than children to be poor, but the picture varies according to which 'equivalence scales' we use to compare the incomes of different kinds of family.

Pensioner poverty declined in the 1970s, due to increases in the retirement pension. But in the 1980s, many groups were affected by the great rise in poverty. Unemployment and lone parenthood soared, and the risk of poverty was very high for both of these groups. Today unemployment is lower but there are many households with no adult in work, and child poverty has become a major problem. There is now no single clear cause of poverty but there is general concern about incentives to work, with the introduction of measures to 'make work pay' and greater financial support for children (see chapter 6).

Is there still a life cycle of poverty?
Rowntree's life cycle of poverty, one of his key concepts which had an enduring impact on social security policy in the

twentieth century, was discussed in chapter 2. Here we attempt to examine how it changed over the century. He illustrated the life cycle with the diagram shown in box 1 in chapter 2. It is unclear how Rowntree constructed his diagram. It appears to incorporate some adjustment for changing family size (or equivalisation) over the life cycle since the poverty line is constant across the age range. Since Rowntree was at that stage not conversant or confident with sampling methods, it seems unlikely that he was familiar with more sophisticated and recent statistical procedures. It seems likely that he drew his diagram without specific data, impressionistically by hand, to illustrate the life cycle he had observed and discussed. Since neither the data nor the researchers are any longer available, we shall never know.

For comparison, the modern extent of a life cycle of poverty has been explored, based an actual data, with results shown in figure 7. There is still, despite extensive lifetime redistribution of income through the social security and tax systems, a significant variation of average income levels over the life cycle. As can be seen, the extent of poverty is highest among children and older people. This pattern is not very different from what Rowntree found although there is not now the fall in income level and rise in poverty associated with the period of having many dependent children when aged between 25 and 45.

A further difference between lifetime experiences of poverty is that between men and women. In 1899 women made up about 60 per cent of all poor adults. In 2001/02 women made up 54 per cent of those aged 16 and over who were poor. Thus women were and are more likely to be poor. However, as stressed in Chapter 2 and considered by Lewis and Piachaud (1992), it is misleading to refer to a 'feminisation' of poverty in Britain – poverty has for a long time been feminised.

Social and economic changes
In this section some of the most significant and striking changes over the century are considered. It is not possible to assess the

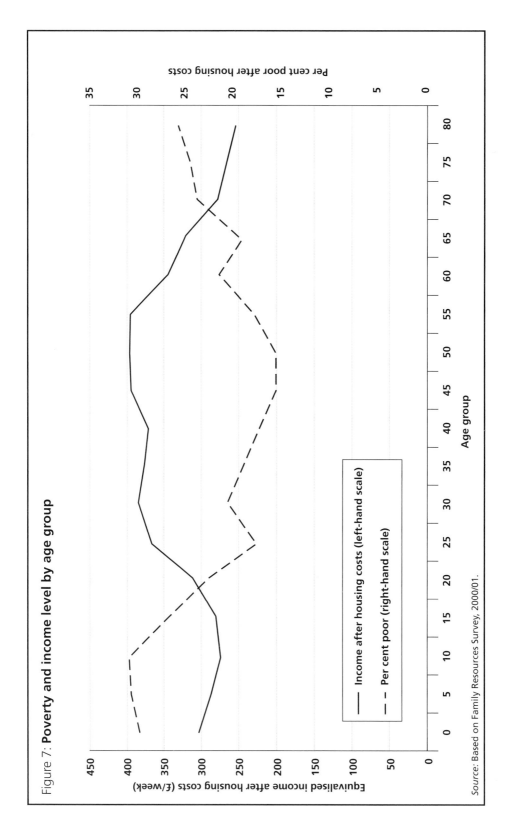

Figure 7: **Poverty and income level by age group**

Source: Based on Family Resources Survey, 2000/01.

Table 4: **Age distribution of population, York**

Age	1901 (%)	2001 (%)
Under 5	11.2	5.2
5–9	10.1	5.4
10–14	10.1	5.9
15–17	6.0	3.4
18–24	14.7	11.0
25–44	28.8	28.7
45–59	11.9	18.6
60–74	5.9	13.7
75–84	1.1	6.1
85+	0.2	2.1
All ages	100.0	100.0

Note: 1901 data are for York County Borough, 2001 data for York Urban Authority.
Source: Census 1901, p. 191; Census 2001, table KS02.

impact of each of these changes on poverty but they do indicate how some things have changed a lot, and some not very much.

Population

York's total population increased over the century – as did Britain's – but, owing to boundary changes, it is hard to be sure how much. What is more relevant is the changing age structure. This is shown in table 4.

What is apparent is the extent of the 'ageing' of the population. In 1901 nearly one-third (31.4 per cent) was aged under 15 compared to one-sixth (16.5 per cent) in 2001; those aged 60 or over tripled from 7.2 per cent in 1901 to 21.9 per cent in 2001. There has been a dramatic fall in infant and child mortality, and those reaching middle age live longer.

The proportions of the population who were unmarried (40 per cent), married (52 per cent) and widowed (8 per cent) were little different across the century but each category had changed.

In 2001 one-fifth of the currently unmarried were divorced, one seventh of those married had been remarried, and 4 per cent of those who were still legally married were separated.[3]

A third, clear change in population was that in 1901 0.9 per cent of York's population was born outside the British Isles; in 2001 this had increased to 4.7 per cent.[4]

Economic activity, occupations and earnings

The extent of economic activity and the principal occupations of all adults (up to age 75 in 2001) are shown in table 5.

Among adult men there has been a striking fall in economic activity: only 1 in 14 was not engaged in an occupation in 1901 compared with 1 in 3 in 2001. Among women the opposite has occurred, with a rise from 31 per cent to 56 per cent in occupations. There was a greater difference between unmarried women and women who were married or widowed in 1901; 61 per cent of the former were in employment compared to 10 per cent of the latter. In 2001 this difference was much smaller, with over 70 per cent of married women with dependent children being economically active. The combination of the decline in employment among older workers, due to the growth in both early retirement and numbers on disability benefits, and the rise in female employment have had major consequences for the distribution of incomes.

While economic activity changed greatly, the pattern of earnings was much more stable. The share of employment income in gross domestic product remained remarkably constant – between 70 and 80 per cent – through the twentieth century. The dispersion of earnings changed very little in the first 70 years of the century (Thatcher, 1968); it fell during the 1970s and then increased from 1980 until the end of the century (Atkinson, 2000).

Table 5: **Economic activity and occupations, York, 1901 and 2001**

	Males		Females	
	1901 *14+*	*2001* *16–74*	*1901* *14+*	*2001* *16–74*
Percentages engaged in occupations	92.6	66.9	31.4	56.2
Distribution of occupations (% of all active)				
Manufacturing	7.9	18.9	n.s.	6.4
Transport and communication	17.8	9.4	n.s.	4.1
Motor trade	–	14.8	–	19.0
Construction	14.3	11.3	n.s.	1.8
Food, lodging and domestic services	12.1	5.0	55.0	8.6
Social services	n.s.	10.6	n.s.	32.6
Other (incl. n.s.)	55.8	38.9	45.0	33.9

Note: n.s. is not specified.
Source: Census 1901, table 35A; Census 2001, table KS11b and c.

Pattern of expenditure

The distribution of expenditure in 1899 was most fully analysed by Rowntree only for those on the lowest earnings; the results are compared with results for a similar proportion of households in 2001/02 in table 6.

By far the most striking change is that in food expenditure. In 1899 poorer households spent over half their income on food: after rent, fuel and lighting, they had less than one quarter to spend on other things. By contrast in 2001/02 nearly half was spent on other things and food represented only one sixth of total expenditure. Only 12 per cent was spent on non-basic other things in 1899 whereas this had grown to 40 per cent in 2001/02.

Housing

Housing circumstances have changed drastically. First, there has been a change in tenure. Rowntree described the working class population of York in 1899 as tenants – without exception they

Table 6: **Distribution of expenditure (%)**

Distribution of expenditure	1899 Class I [1]	2001/02 Bottom quintile group[2]
Food	51	17
Rent	18	28[3]
Fuel and lighting	9	6
Clothing	6	6
Insurance and sick cover	4	3
Other	12	40
Total	100	100

Notes:
1 Weekly earnings under 26 shillings. These constitute about 20% of all households.
2 Average of lowest and second decile groups.
3 See section on housing.
Source: Rowntree (1901), p. 244; Family Spending 2001/02, Office for National Statistics, 2003.

rented their accommodation. Others in the 'servant-keeping class' owned their own homes but he assumed that this did not happen among the working class. In 2001 in York the tenure groups were:

Owned outright	32.1%
Owned with mortgage	40.3%
Rented from local authority	10.5%
Rented from housing association	4.6%
Rented from private landlord	8.7%
Other	3.8%

Renting is now confined to one quarter of households and many of the poor in 2001 are owner-occupiers.

A second major change has been in the quality of housing. In 1899 Rowntree found that over 20 per cent of houses in York had to share a closet with another house, some sharing with five or more other houses. These were not water closets but mostly midden privies, essentially holes in the ground. Not all houses had their own water supply, with 15 per cent sharing a water tap.

Third, the density of living has been greatly reduced. It is not that houses are much larger: in 1899 there were about 5 rooms per household, compared to 5.3 in 2001 (although rooms may be larger and what is counted as a room has changed slightly, making precise comparison impossible). But the number in each household has fallen markedly from a mean of 4 in 1899 to 2.4 in 2001. Whereas in 1899 nearly all households had more than one member and most had dependent children, in 2001 nearly a third of households had only one member, of which half were pensioners, and only one fifth had dependent children.

Rents in 1899 amounted to 18 per cent of total expenditure of the poorest fifth, as shown in table 6. Even in Rowntree's highest income group rents were 13 per cent of total expenditure. The rent figure for 2001/02 in table 6 is based on gross rent: taking into account housing benefit, rebates and allowances, net rent for the lowest quintile amounted to only 6 per cent of expenditure.

Thus for poorer tenants the net cost of housing is now a much lower burden than in Rowntree's day, but rent levels vary widely. Similarly, among owner-occupiers the cost of mortgage interest is highly variable. In sum, while the quality of housing has improved enormously, the variation in its cost has greatly increased.

Consumer durables

Alongside the extension of owner-occupation, the acquisition of consumer durables has increased the capital ownership of virtually all households. In analysing consumer durables no comparison is possible with 1899 since Rowntree did not analyse their ownership – in most cases for the very good reason that the products had yet to be invented. In 2001 the proportions of households in Britain with different consumer durables were as shown in table 7.

Table 7: **Access to consumer durables, bottom income quintile group, 2001/02 (%)**

Colour television	98
Washing machine	93
Central heating	89
Telephone	85
Video recorder	86
Microwave	83
Mobile phone	70
Car or van	59
Tumble dryer	49
Home computer	42

Note: Table shows bottom fifth by net equivalised income after housing costs.
Source: DWP (2003a), appendix 3, table 3.1.

The majority of the population had access to most of the durables listed. In the case of cars there was more variation in the distribution. In York in 2001 one-quarter (27.3 per cent) of households had no car (or van), half (48.6 per cent) had one car, one fifth (20.1 per cent) had two cars, and 1 in 25 (3.9 per cent) had three or more cars.

The mass ownership of consumer durables, including by those in the lowest fifth of income levels, represents an economic and social transformation. How far they all improve quality of life is open to debate. In the case of cars, the consequences of non-ownership in terms of mobility and lack of access to amenities, cheaper shopping and much else are important. Lack of a car is far more common among poorer households. But in terms of many of the accoutrements of modern life in Britain the poor are not now far behind those better off.

Dependence on one earner

In 1899 the earnings of households from paid work averaged 32 shillings a week. This was the total income for most households (excluding payments by lodgers). The earnings were provided by:

Head of household (almost all male)   82%
Male supplementary earners   13%
Female supplementary earners   5%

Thus over four-fifths of household incomes came from one earner – literally the breadwinner.

In 2001 the numbers of economically active persons in households were as follows:[5]

0   32%
1   28%
2   31%
3   7%
4+   2%

Far more households have two or more earners than in 1899 but in addition far more have no earner at all. The widening of the distribution of economic activity is the greatest single change that has increased income inequality.

Poor relief, social security and redistribution

At the start of 1901 the York Poor Law Union provided at public expense for 492 people in York Workhouse and for 1,049 through 'outdoor relief' – payments to people living in their own homes. 'Outdoor relief' provided for 1.4 per cent of the population at a cost of £5,950 (Rowntree, 1901, pp. 365–76); thus, outdoor relief amounted to at most 0.4 per cent of income from earnings in York.[6]

In 2001/02 in Britain, one tenth of households received over half their income from income related benefits.[7] While Income Support amounted to 1.4 per cent of gross incomes, a more relevant figure however is total state spending on all cash benefits, which amounted to 12.7 per cent of gross income.[8]

The role of the state in providing incomes and relieving poverty has changed beyond any possible imagining of Seebohm Rowntree.

Despite the tiny levels, by modern standards, of expenditure on poor relief, some of the concerns then are all too familiar now. In the final paragraph of his study, Rowntree wrote:

There is no doubt a considerable amount of abuse in connection with the giving of out-relief – persons receiving it who are not really destitute, or who have relations who could and should maintain them, whilst others receive it only to spend it upon drink. Not a few such cases have come under the notice of the writer during the course of the present investigation. This does not, however, necessarily, nor in fact does it at all, reflect upon the honesty or ability of the relieving officers. But the number of these is inadequate, there being only two for the whole city. The abuse points, however, to the necessity of appointing a Superintendent Relieving Officer, for it must be borne in mind that ill-administered outdoor relief not only entails financial waste, but has a serious demoralizing effect upon the community.

The next chapter turns to the solutions, albeit partial, that were developed over the last century, both in attempting to reduce poverty, and to cope with such concerns.

Part II
A century of policy responses

5 Poverty policy from 1900 to the 1970s

Howard Glennerster

Twentieth century Britain inherited a unique poor law tradition, much derided and much misunderstood. Reformers in the first half of the century tried to transform that poor law tradition into a social insurance based model. With the Beveridge Report of 1942 and the legislative changes of the 1940s, they seemed to have succeeded. Yet that was not to be. The comprehensive post-war social insurance schemes never eliminated poverty or major dependence on the old public assistance tradition. At the end of the century a new modern version of targeted aid to the poor emerged, including supplementing the wages of the working poor.

As Jose Harris has put it:

> *From the 1900s onwards . . . the poor law system in Britain was continually supplemented, and appeared eventually to be ousted, by a series of alternative income-support policies based largely on social insurance; the climax of this process with the formal 'abolition of the poor laws' in 1948 was felt by many to be a defining moment in Britain's post-war history. Yet from the early 1960s, welfare structures covertly bequeathed from the poor laws began to re-emerge in British social policy as the major instrument of publicly-funded income support; at the end of the century Britain once again had the most profoundly poor-type welfare system of any country in Europe. What*

accounts for the strange survival of this supposedly much-hated institution?'
(2002, p. 410)

In order to try to answer that question we need to reflect briefly on the significance of that poor law tradition in Britain.

The roots of poverty relief: A distinct tradition

The First Tudor poor laws date from 1495 when the dilemmas posed by the poor were a topic of moral and political debate across Europe (Innes, 1998, 1999; Michielse, 1990; Slack, 1988, 1990). What balance should be struck between private charity and public concern for good order?

Prior to that time the predominant view was that the poor were a proper charitable concern of the faithful. Monasteries, almshouses, guilds, donations to the poor of the parish were private activities. The state confined itself to punishing vagabonds.

Rising concern for and fear of the poor and the need to think rationally about some organised responses to poverty were argued by Erasmus and Juan Luis Vives (1492–1540) and pioneered in both Catholic and Protestant European cities from Ypres, Strasbourg and Geneva to Lyon and Tudor London.

In contrast to the previous system of Christian charity and the medieval view of poverty, the main characteristics of the new approach to poor relief can be summarised as follows: the social salvation of the recipients rather than the spiritual salvation of the donors took precedence; secular rather than church authorities became the central agents of poor relief; the maze of independent institutions was replaced by a central institution, the 'common chest'; begging was prohibited, no longer an accepted practice of the paupers Christi; and the central concern was no longer benevolence but the subjection of

*the poor to a systematic and disciplinarian program of
education and improvement.*
(Michielse, 1990, pp. 2–3)

In fact, the tension between deeply held Christian humanist
ideals and a realist appreciation that charity could go too far,
creating a pauper population, has been recurrent in debates
about poverty policy right up to the present.

If these innovations and ideas were European-wide, England
came up with an unusual solution. A national framework of
duties was placed on parishes in their treatment of the poor in
1597 and 1601, though with considerable local discretion about
the means employed. Such an approach was not so different
from some other countries but the general power to levy a tax
to meet the expenses of poor relief was. The fact that this
taxing power was almost universally adopted by local parishes
meant England was following a distinctive route. It was much
criticised as taking away the personal responsibility to give and
leading to the excessive relief of the poor. It was wrong, critics
argued, because it embodied a 'right to relief' (Innes, 2002).

Poor relief took less than 1 per cent of the GDP in 1696 and
rose to 2 per cent by 1800. The numbers covered probably rose
from about 3.5 per cent of the population in 1700 to 8 per cent
by mid century and 14 per cent by 1800 (Slack, 1990). It was the
consequent cost and the very existence of a national legislative
framework that attracted the attention of leading social
scientists of the day – not just Adam Smith and Malthus but a
whole range of serious commentators, political economists and
statisticians (Blaug, 1963; Dunkley, 1982; Horne, 1986; Innes,
1999). The concern was not just with the misguided actions of a
few local burghers, as critics saw it. It was a national issue.
Westminster chose to address the early nineteenth century
critics by tightening the rules of access in the famous 1834
reforms, but *not* by revoking the ultimate right to relief as
some had urged. It was *outdoor* relief, cash given outside the
demeaning and rigorous workhouse that was frowned upon.

The 1834 Act took poor relief out of the hands of amateurs, creating a body of professional staff who served the new amalgamated parish 'unions'. It set out a national test of need, requiring relief for the able-bodied only in the workhouse, setting out regulations for the conduct of those institutions. The level of relief was also set. It should be lower than the standard of life that could be gained from the lowest wage the market would offer outside. This principle of 'less eligibility' was not new, but it was given its classic articulation. It would be wrong too to give the impression that these principles were universally implemented. Local traditions, ideologies of relief almost, the revenue available from the local rate and local economic circumstances differed widely. The Webbs made this point but there now is a vast modern literature on local poor law diversity (see Webb and Webb, 1929; Kidd, 1999; King, 2000, for summaries).

The significance of national legislation and national guidelines should not be underplayed, however. After a strong upward trend in poor relief spending that had reached £7 million in 1830, slightly down on 1820, it fell to £4.6 million by 1840 despite a growing population, and the scale of relief in

The 'Poor Law divorce', 1846. When people entered the workhouse, married couples were forced to live and work separately.

relation to size of the population went on falling until the late part of the century. Moreover, in its concern to contain the scale of relief, central government created the most centralised national pattern of poverty relief anywhere in Europe. A powerful group of poor law inspectors began to shape local administration and did so through to the 1930s. This involved 'a degree of centralised bureaucratic control largely unknown in the poor law systems of mainland Europe' (Harris, 2002, p. 420). There was still much local variation and variation in treatment by types of client – a hierarchy of 'deservingness'. But it was an increasingly centrally regulated safety net that became, by stages, a nationally administered and calculated safety net by 1948. This was again a step ahead of European countries and North America. It was to have important implications for the eventual fate of the social insurance model in the twentieth century.

Those writing accounts of the history of social policy as recently as the 1970s (Fraser, 1973) could present the story as one of gradual 'progress' – the Poor Law in all its evil forms gave way, in gradual stages, to a growing range of social insurance schemes that secured households against the main causes of poverty. All this was underpinned by a comprehensive safety net that caught the few who fell through. This insurance system had its faults but they were being systematically put right. The state had learned how to prevent long term unemployment. That was the story in outline. Yet, as the quote from Professor Harris with which we began shows, this is not a storyline modern social historians can adopt. Yet, at least until 1948, it seemed a plausible account.

Escaping the Poor Law? 1900–48

The Royal Commission on the Poor Laws which sat in the early part of the last century reflected, in its famous majority and minority reports (1909), the clash of ideas about the causes of poverty we discussed in our opening section – a clash that was embodied in the formidable personalities of two women commissioners, Helen Bosanquet and Beatrice Webb. Both believed that some of the poor were beyond relief and that those on relief could not just be left to do as they pleased in seeking or not seeking work or in the care of children. But the majority view was that poverty was essentially a moral problem that lay with the poor and it was exacerbated by the lax and overgenerous way in which the Poor Law was being administered. Part of the solution lay in active help and counselling for those entrapped by it. But that required tougher action with those who would not respond. We can see clear parallels with modern debates about welfare reform. The minority report saw the causes of poverty as largely the result of basic structural factors in the economy and argued that provision for the poor should simply become part of a range of services for the whole community like health, education and child care. This proved a durable thread in the debate over the coming century. The minority report became the centrepiece of a campaign to abolish the Poor Law.

The elderly

The first group to escape the old Poor Law was the able-bodied elderly. The reasons lay not just in a concern for their deserving welfare but in a determination to bear down on the able-bodied feckless who were seen as a cause of rising poor law costs. Older people had always been relatively well treated by poor law authorities but posed a problem if the rising costs of poor relief were to be contained. The changing industrial structure of the country, the political economy of poor relief and the newly politically organised working class all contributed. In rural areas it was not unusual for men and women to continue working part-time in less physically demanding ways well into their sixties and early seventies. Old-established family firms may have moved workers into less onerous jobs as they aged (Macnicol, 1998). The more competitive international environment of the late nineteenth and early twentieth century and the new industry of the time meant that employers were less able or prepared to keep men on much beyond their peak productive period. (We were to see comparable effects in the 1980s.) Yet life expectancy was growing. The risks of poverty in old age were growing because most workers had little opportunity to save significant sums for themselves and their wives. Local ratepayers were unhappy at the rising costs. If the central government took on this responsibility, they would be relieved. Trade unions believed older workers posed a threat to jobs. They also genuinely believed that a decent pension was a fair reward for a lifetime of work.

Pensions paid out of taxes became a rallying cry of the new radical Liberals as well as the new Labour movement and social reformers including Booth. This solution also appealed to those who wanted to see a more decisive return to the principles of 1834. Detach the more favoured elderly from the Poor Law and a more rigorous application of the workhouse test would become easier. The old guard in the Charity Organisation Society did not see things that way. They saw any extension of state relief as undermining individual independence. But this combination of rather unusual allies and the election of a Liberal government in 1906 produced the first important 'welfare' legislation of the twentieth century, though it would pose increasing long term problems, as we shall see.

The Old Age Pensions Act 1908 *was* a radical and popular measure. All those who had been continuously resident in the UK for 20 years before they were 70 could qualify subject to a means test. The pension was 5 shillings a week (10s for a couple) and was reduced if income rose above £21 a year. There were all kinds of bad behaviour disqualifications, such as convictions for drunkenness, which were later dropped, and the residence requirement was shortened. Moreover, 94 per cent of pensions were for the full amount, showing the limited incomes or savings people had. This was the first anti-poverty measure to be financed out of central taxation and marked the beginning of the trail to the modern welfare state. But it also

THE PHILANTHROPIC HIGHWAYMAN.

Mr. Lloyd-George. "I'LL MAKE 'EM PITY THE AGED POOR!"

A 1908 cartoon from Punch magazine showing Lloyd George as a highwayman, collecting funds for the new old age pensions.

posed dilemmas that are still with us. The pension was means tested. It was a boon to those who had never had the chance to save. But what would it do to the saving habits of those in the next generation? Those who had saved, or been members of a friendly society or other scheme, lost any benefit as their state pension was docked pound for pound. Pressure grew to remove the means test or raise the income limit for the pension, lower the age at which it could be drawn and make it more generous, especially as the pension lost value with the inflation of the war years. The Treasury began to worry that it had let loose a tiger that would eat up its revenue.

One way out was favoured by many Liberals, the Treasury itself and the 'new' Conservatives led by Chamberlain. The strategy was to adopt the route taken for the sick and unemployed in 1911 – 'National Insurance'. Calls on the Exchequer would be limited by making the worker and his employer responsible for the cost of pensions in the long term. Pressure for higher pensions would be tempered by the knowledge that this would result in higher contributions from existing workers. The costs would not be passed on to the well-off income tax payer. On the other hand, rights to benefit would be earned by virtue of the contribution record, not a means test, which would have advantages for the elderly person. More than one committee began work on the issue and the failure of the minority Labour government of 1924 to come up with any alternative left the new Conservative government with the opportunity to take the decisive step towards a social insurance model – the 1925 Widows', Orphans' and Old Age Contributions Act.

A pension would be paid at 65 to all those who had been contributing to the National Insurance schemes for sickness and unemployment and to wives and widows of contributors. The old age pension scheme for those aged 70 would remain but would no longer be means tested. In 1940 the old age pension was paid from the age of 60 for women who were insured in their own right or where the husband had reached 65. The 1908

Old age pensioners marched from St Paul's to the House of Commons in November 1938 to demand an increase in pensions from 10 shillings to £1 a week.

scheme had been good for women. Right to benefit was based on age and residence. Married women received the same sum as the husband. Under the new scheme women became covered dependent on the husband's work record.

None of these measures removed all old people from poverty and the Poor Law, however. Many women who were single or who had been deserted, divorced or separated were on poor relief, as were those of both sexes who were not covered by a full contribution record or whose rents brought them below the means test level.

Only about 10 per cent of pensioners claimed public assistance. But in 1940, yielding to growing pressure for increased pensions across the board, the Treasury responded by suggesting a much cheaper solution – an increase in the supplement the poorest pensioners could receive on public assistance. This was adopted in that year. Old age and widow pensioners could receive support from the national agency set up to provide assistance to the unemployed several years earlier, renamed the Assistance Board. The Treasury was convinced that few would be eligible. In fact 1.25 million applied in the first two months. Freed from the stigma associated with the local public assistance committees, more old people were prepared to apply. This and the earlier creation of the Unemployment Assistance Board, as well as the later creation of the National Assistance Board, were decisive moves. Faced with mounting all party pressure to raise pensions for all, the Treasury was able to persuade the government, as it was to persuade succeeding ones, that a much cheaper and more effective strategy lay in relieving the plight of the poorest alone through a national agency applying a national test of need. It was to emerge as the winning strategy of the latter half of the twentieth century.

Widows

Widows were the next most blameless group. They could least of all be blamed for their poverty. Male age-related mortality rates were a third higher than female rates at the turn of the century (Kiernan, Land and Lewis, 1998). Widows' causes had been successfully championed in the United States at the end of the nineteenth century in a political climate very hostile to federal government action. In a situation where most women were dependent on a man's wage and premature male death was common, widowhood was a major risk and one that commanded public sympathy. Widows' pensions were introduced for the wives of insured workers in the 1925 Act but the test of respectability remained. 'Evidence of a new relationship undermined a widow's claim to support because it was assumed the man involved would support her' (Brooks, 1986).

Sickness

Legitimate absence from work for short term ill health was again a deserving cause. It was something better off workers had clubbed together to support. Simple statistics suggested larger groups would be less vulnerable, hence the growth of some large national friendly societies. The fact that workers were paying for each others' sickness absence meant there was a strong incentive to police false claims or overlong absence. It was this feature that Lloyd George thought would help prevent abuse of any national scheme. Moreover, politically the friendly societies were both powerful and useful. They had the spread of administrative capacity and were organised to do the job of giving out cash benefits to the sick and paying for treatment by the general practitioner. They would need to be incorporated in the administration of any national scheme. So, too, would the profit-making industrial insurance companies that provided insurance to cover the costs of burial on a large scale to the working class and who promised to make things difficult if they were left out.

This set a pattern for later social legislation. State provision was built around and accommodated existing non-governmental provision, though in the process it often stifled or restricted it. In many ways the rather complex administration of a state benefit through very varied not-for-profit and profit-making organisations worked remarkably well (Whiteside, 1983). It was, however, seen as deeply unfair by those who were not in employment or insured occupations, and who were excluded. Small societies and those whose members were sickest could not provide the range of benefits others could. The rising level of unemployment put pressure on the finances of the schemes and was to lead to many losing their rights until the unemployed gained rights to medical benefit. Whiteside concludes: 'In short and simple terms [in a work based insurance scheme] the best lives, and the highest wage earners, win the best treatment; the system penalises those not in the labour market and those dependent on them including the unemployed' (1983, p. 191).

Homeless men at a soup kitchen in 1924. Lack of employment was an increasing cause of poverty during the 1920s and 1930s.

The unemployed

In good times at the turn of the century Rowntree had not found unemployment to be a major reason for poverty in York. In the 1920s and especially the 1930s it was to become the major scourge. The major industries that had been the main exporters in the nineteenth century struggled after the First World War and through the 1920s. They were then hit by the world economic crisis after 1929. This reached into many people's lives and affected those who had never had to undergo the experience of poverty or the indignity of relying on the local public assistance committee.

But this experience was not uniform. New industries were growing in the south. Prices fell, new mass produced consumer goods began to appear and those in work, especially in these new industries, did reasonably well. Most people were better off in 1939 than they had been a decade earlier.

'Unemployment' rates in 1932 varied for the different regions of the country between 36 per cent in Wales and 13 per cent in London and the South East. By the mid 1930s the

75

disparity was even more striking, with unemployment rates in some towns in the depressed areas revealing tragic stories of the decay and impoverishment of whole communities; places such as Brynmawr, Dowlais, Jarrow, Gateshead, Greenock and Motherwell had almost three-quarters of the insured population out of work in 1934, while other parts of the country were experiencing almost boom conditions (Stevenson and Cook, 1979, p. 5). Special areas received rather late and inadequate assistance, but this was the beginning of what we today would call area based policy.

Economic theory was turned upside down. Unemployment was clearly not temporary or self correcting. Government came to see it had a responsibility to affect the total level of demand. The Budget of 1942 was the first to recognise this responsibility.

The scale of unemployment shook the localised system of public assistance to the core and transformed it. The means test

The Jarrow Crusade, 1936. Marching 300 miles from Jarrow in the north-east to London, the marchers wanted to highlight the poverty and mass unemployment they and their families were facing.

and the local administration of poor relief became the focus of bitter working class protest. Local areas could not support the burden out of local taxes. In 1931 the Treasury had to take responsibility for those who were unemployed long term and who had lost their insurance rights. A national Unemployment Assistance Board took over responsibility for this group in 1935 and administered the first nationally funded safety net for the unemployed, not as a way of being more generous or equitable but to contain spending. The administration of welfare became the object of huge organised protests that did succeed in reversing benefit cuts. The logic of national responsibility inherent in the Tudor poor law had finally come home to roost.

Family and child poverty
The central feature of Rowntree's original diagnosis, the particular needs of families with children, had not been addressed despite the analytical and advocacy work of Rathbone (1917, 1924), many in the suffragette movement and the conversion of key reformers like Beveridge to family allowances and Rowntree's minimum wage proposal. The issue *had* been addressed in France and the reasons are interesting. The British trade unions saw children as a useful bargaining chip in arguing for a living family wage. French employers saw the advantages of denying that lever. If employers collectively redistributed the rewards of labour to reflect the number of children in the family, pressure to raise the total wage bill might be mitigated. The pro-family attitude of the Catholic Church and the pro-natalist stance of government were conducive to this strategy succeeding.

> In 1932, the state extended these benefits by requiring all employers in industry to affiliate to one of the private, business-controlled funds (caisses de compensation) that had been set up to equalise the costs of such benefits across firms in particular sectors or regions. Family allowances were extended to agricultural workers and

Children drinking milk at school in 1938. Local authorities were empowered to provide free milk from 1921; in 1946 the School Milk Act ordered that all pupils under 18 should rececive one-third of a pint of milk per day.

small farmers in the years immediately before the Second World War.
(Pedersen, 1993, p. 17)

France thus made far more extensive and explicit provision for dependent children in the interwar period than did Britain. Yet it did not do so in the way Eleanor Rathbone would have hoped.

> *If we can characterise British social policy as the articulation of a male breadwinner logic of welfare, French policies come to rest on a very different logic, which I will term 'parental' . . . Put simply, while male-breadwinner policies compensate men for dependent women and children during legitimate interruptions of earnings, states with parental policies compensate adults for dependent children irrespective of earnings or need.*
> (Pedersen, 1993, pp. 17–18)

The Beveridge Report and the end of poverty?

So as the Second World War approached the gradual evolution of a social insurance state was well underway (see table 8).

It was this complex system of multiple and partial social insurance schemes that Beveridge was appointed to sort out. But Beveridge interpreted his brief in a much more ambitious way (Harris, 1997). He saw his role as setting out a programme of reform – 'a social plan' – that would, once and for all, abolish poverty. In those heady post-war days many thought this had been, or would shortly be, accomplished.

Beveridge convinced himself, reading Rowntree's new study of poverty in York (1941), that a reform of the insurance schemes we have described and their extension to the whole population would be enough to abolish 'want' so long as they

	Unemployment	*Health*	*Old age, widows, orphans*
1914	2,500	13,689	–
1921	11,081	15,165	–
1926	11,774	16,375	17,089
1931	12,500	17,353	18,513
1936	14,580	18,081	19,651
1938	15,395	19,706	20,678

Table 8: **The growth of social insurance (numbers insured in 000s)**

Source: Beveridge (1942), p. 213.

were accompanied by a series of other key changes that went far beyond his brief:

- the ending of long term unemployment through budgetary policy and demand management;
- the creation of a free National Health Service at the point of use;
- family allowances set at a level that would cover the basic costs of the second and subsequent children (for an account of how and why this came to be accepted for reasons that had little to do with poverty relief, see Macnicol, 1980);
- for those who slipped through this comprehensive 'cradle to grave' cover, a new National Assistance Board that would provide a final safety net.

Beveridge's notes (found in his own papers) on Rowntree's book make his logic clear: 'the causes of poverty directly amenable to social insurance accounted for one quarter of

Family Allowance day in London, 1946. The allowance was paid to the mother in order to make sure the money was spent on the children. When it was introduced, mothers received 5 shillings a week for each child apart from the eldest.

primary poverty in 1899 and for five-sixths of the primary poverty in 1936' (Evans and Glennerster, 1993). These contingencies, unemployment, old age, widowhood and large families, sickness including industrial injuries, could be covered by a range of insurance benefits covered by a single national insurance contribution, he argued. It is notable that if Beveridge had used Rowntree's more generous measure of the human needs of labour, low wages would have formed a larger part of the explanation.

Benefits would be set at a level sufficient to raise all those on benefit above a 'minimum needed for subsistence'. Beveridge suggested taking Rowntree's primary poverty line as a marker for this subsistence level. To which Rowntree objected, though he compromised downwards from his human needs of labour measure to help Beveridge keep his costs down (Veit-Wilson, 1994). In his report Beveridge gave himself a let-out clause: 'If social policy should demand benefits on a higher scale than subsistence, the whole level of benefit and contribution rates could be raised without affecting the structure of the scheme' (1942, para. 27).

Universal family allowances would ideally be set at the cost of bringing up a child – they never were, as we shall see. No one would have to face the costs of medical care or education. Most people would therefore be taken out of poverty. Only a small number would have to be caught by the National Assistance safety net. The logic seemed elegant and it has dominated much mainstream thinking on the left of politics ever since. But the utopia was never to be. The benefit levels set were never enough to raise those wholly dependent on them above the levels set by the National Assistance scales, in their turn linked to the bottom of the wage scale, let alone more generous notions. Family allowances were left to stagnate in real terms and were never set at a level sufficient to provide for a child's basic needs. Some have blamed politicians, the Treasury and powerful economic and private insurance interests.[1] But at root the logic and the political dynamics of the scheme itself were at fault.

For 30 or more years after the national insurance scheme was founded in its modern post-Beveridge form Labour governments sought to remedy some of its defects while Conservative governments resisted, never having accepted the cost consequences its full logic demanded. Nor, it has to be said, did Labour governments, in practice.

From Beveridge to the 1970s
Fundamental flaws in the Beveridge model

Some of the flaws were evident at the time. The cost of what Beveridge wanted to do was simply not acceptable to the Treasury then or subsequently. In trying to squeeze the package into an acceptable cash constraint the integrity of the package fell apart. A few examples illustrate this:

- The assumption was that setting universal flat rate insurance benefits at Rowntree's primary poverty level would lift all those on such benefits out of poverty. This ignored the wide diversity of rent levels faced by people in different parts of the country, as Rowntree and others pointed out (Glennerster and Evans, 1994). Excluding rent from his calculation meant that most poor people would still be subject to a means test by the National Assistance Board to meet their rent. Housing Benefit now covers the rental housing costs of the poor but it does so at the cost of including a wide range of households in a means tested poverty trap. Sixty years on we have not solved the problem that defeated Beveridge.
- If the model were to work, it had to work for pensioners and it did not (Macnicol, 1998). Giving a universal flat rate pension meant spending most money on the non-poor and limited the generosity possible given the budgetary limits the Treasury was setting. If the funds were not to come from taxation (as Beveridge agreed they should not in the long run), the funds had to come from a flat rate insurance contribution. This would bear heavily on the poor. Beveridge stuck to the notion of a flat rate contribution established at the beginning of the

century as a way of restricting the scope of the potential cost. The Treasury was determined the scheme should not be a burden on the general taxpayer. The trade unions argued that the costs on the low paid should not be excessive. What gave was the benefit level. Though the pension proposed by Beveridge was raised by the 1945 Labour government, the essential problem was never solved by it or by successive governments. The attempt to introduce benefits related to previous wages came too late. The political dynamics set up by the initial low rates of pension proved irreversible (see below).

- The scheme confined married women to the status of dependents. Single women would be treated as contributors like men. Marriage was an insurance contract, Beveridge argued. A woman's needs were met by her husband. They should be treated as a unit and she would be insured, as would her children, as dependents of her husband. Rights to benefit relied on the husband's work. Women's incentives to work, especially for low pay, were small. Since Beveridge was so concerned with raising the birth rate this was a virtue for him, but it was to lay up serious problems for the future.
- The disabled who were not disabled at work or by war were not included in his scheme of things.

Now some of these flaws were capable of remedies. The basis of the contributions and benefits could become income related, as was to be the case in other European countries and America. Women could be treated as insured in their own right. Special tax based schemes for the disabled could be introduced. Benefit levels could be made more generous. All these were to become the stuff of successive attempts to reform the national insurance system from 1958 to 1975. In the end they too failed.

Dynamic flaws

The political dynamics set up by the Beveridge plan were to prove disastrous to any coherent poverty programme in the next decades.

- State benefit levels were constrained by what the poorest could contribute – deliberately so, many would argue. It was one of the attractions of the flat rate model to the Treasury. This meant that skilled workers, let alone the middle class, never saw the state pension scheme as sufficiently generous to rely on in old age. They negotiated their own occupational pension alternatives. This created a powerful set of interests that opposed going down the road of a generous wage-related alternative. When the Labour Party began to discuss a wage related alternative, moving to a copy of the US, Swedish and German models, in the 1950s, the trade unions were some of the strongest opponents. Private pension companies had a powerful voice and no state scheme could be introduced which threatened them. The basic Beveridge pension scheme became less important to the median voter and to the poor. When Mrs Thatcher's government broke the link between benefit rates and average earnings in the 1980s (see chapter 6) it did so largely with political impunity.

- When the post-war pension scheme was re-examined in the 1950s, and on subsequent occasions, the killer question was: why should we spend a lot of money raising the basic pension or other benefits for most people when the poorest are already catered for by the National Assistance scheme? The Wilson government of 1964 did significantly raise the level of the basic pension and other basic benefits. But it came under political pressure to raise the level of National Assistance too. Otherwise the poorest, and especially poor elderly people, would not gain. So a very expensive policy 'floated off' very few people from means tests.

- The 1974 Labour government again raised the basic pension, this time by 30 per cent in money terms and 12 per cent in real terms. It also brought in the State Earnings Related Pension Scheme. This was the last attempt to make the universal National Insurance model work. But it came too late. Mrs Thatcher came to power and both reduced the generosity of the scheme and encouraged many not to join it, with significant tax relief for joining private pension schemes instead. There was no large body of middle class pensioners who saw it as in their interests to defend the state scheme, as there has been in the US.

Poverty disappears and reappears

It took time for the weaknesses of the post-war settlement to sink in. Compared to the 1930s, the 1940s were indeed an improvement. Rowntree's third study of York (Rowntree and Lavers, 1951) made the case. It was based on a sample survey. Rowntree had at last convinced himself that this was a legitimate method! It was brief. The baseline was again a primary poverty line. The diets of 1936 had been slightly modified and some changes had been made in the estimates of a family's need for clothing, fuel, light and sundries. In 1936, 17.7 per cent of the total population had been below the poverty line. In 1950 the figure was only 1.6 per cent. Old age was the main contributory factor at 68 per cent of the total, and the sick made up 21 per cent. Rowntree and Lavers claimed that without the welfare measures including food subsidies introduced after the Second World War, poverty would have been much higher than it actually was – 25 per cent!

Poverty disappeared from the political radar in the 1950s until the end of the decade, when work on poverty among the elderly resurfaced (Cole and Utting, 1962). Later work on Rowntree's last results threw some doubt on them. Abel-Smith and Townsend (1965) used the national sample provided by the Family Expenditure Survey and updated Rowntree's poverty line in line with prices as a check on their own findings for 1953/54 (see below). They found 5.4 per cent of households in poverty. When Atkinson and colleagues (1981) reanalysed Rowntree's data using the then National Assistance Board scales as the poverty line they found that 14.4 per cent of working class households would have been judged poor.

More recently Hatton and Bailey (2000) have reanalysed the same material to test Rowntree and Lavers' claim that poverty

A mother washes her child in a tin bath in the Salford slums, 1955. Poverty had, however, disappeared from the political radar.

had fallen so dramatically because of the impact of post-war social policy. They find it did fall but by nothing like as much as the earlier study claimed. Rowntree and Lavers claimed that the fall in poverty had been 20 percentage points. Hatton and Bailey suggest it was about 10 percentage points and much of that was the result of food subsidies: 'It is unfortunate that, in the absence of other comparable studies for the 1950s, this produced a somewhat distorted picture of poverty in the early post war period, an impression which took two decades to counteract' (2000, p. 537).

Peter Townsend, as a new young researcher at the Institute for Community Studies, was asked to review Rowntree and

Lavers and was not convinced. It led him to a lifetime of work that has changed the way we think about poverty in most developed economies, with the exception of the United States (Glennerster, 2002).

His central point was that we cannot determine a level of adequacy simply by virtue of some expert calculation of dietary or health needs. Social custom requires that we share cups of tea with neighbours or buy presents for our children at Christmas, even have the occasional pint. It is certainly true that Rowntree recognised this in 1901, as Veit-Wilson (1986) has so forcefully argued. But, as we have shown, the primary poverty notion took on its own life and even Rowntree had in practice abandoned the secondary measure by the time Townsend was writing. To be income poor, in Townsend's terms, was to be excluded, by virtue of one's income, from the normal activities of social life. Townsend thought that it should be possible to construct a list of activities which were the ones that people should be able to undertake if they were not to suffer what we might today call social exclusion (Townsend, 1979). This led to considerable controversy about those activities and whether there was any clear point at which not to be observed doing them could be linked to a poverty line (Piachaud, 1981; Desai and Shah, 1988).

In the interim, however, Townsend and Brian Abel-Smith, his colleague at the London School of Economics, took a pragmatic approach to measurement. Each year Parliament itself made a judgement about what was a minimum acceptable level of income in the UK when it set the National Assistance rates. Why not take that National Assistance rate, plus rent which the Board usually paid, plus some more to cover the extras many people gained as additions to the basic rate, and use that as an indication of 'low levels of living'? To take the crude basic rate would have ignored the fact that some income was 'disregarded' by the Board – small earnings, disability pensions, war savings and the like. Various percentages above the base rate were chosen but the favoured one was 40 per cent above.

They made it clear that this was only a crude first step and that better ways of measuring relative poverty were needed (Abel-Smith and Townsend, 1965, pp. 62–3).

Using an official sample survey of the incomes of families (designed to be used to construct the Retail Price Index), they were able to estimate how many people were living below this poverty line (Abel-Smith and Townsend, 1965). In 1960 they found it was nearly 18 per cent of all households (14 per cent of people). The comparable figure in 1953/54 had been 10 per cent of households and 7.8 per cent of persons. Numbers of elderly poor had grown but, as the authors put it, 'Possibly the most novel finding is the extent of poverty among children. . . . This fact has not been given due emphasis in the policies of political parties' (1965, p. 65).

There was controversy about the report and criticism particularly of the comparisons with 1953/54. National Assistance rates had risen in real terms since 1953, critics said, so of course the numbers of poor had risen. Relative standards of living had risen and, just as with Rowntree, the official poverty line had risen to take that into account, as the authors had argued in the report itself (1965, pp. 16–20).

To meet these criticisms later official measures were to use income relative to a national mean or median income – 40 per cent, 50 per cent of the mean income or more recently 60 per cent of the median.

These technical arguments aside, the wider public, assisted by the work of the Child Poverty Action Group (CPAG), absorbed and accepted the basic argument. The result was to put poverty back on the political map. Social science had 'lifted the curtain' once again so that the comfortable majority had to confront the reality of life at the bottom.

Child poverty became a political issue again. Family allowances had been held constant in cash terms since the early 1950s. They were gradually wasting away in real terms and relative to earnings. They were increased in 1968 as a result of the political pressure CPAG was able to exert across the political spectrum. The standard rate taxpayer had the extra cash fully taxed away. The Conservative government that followed introduced the Family Income Support (FIS) scheme as one of its first measures in 1970 – the alternative the Treasury had favoured all along. It was a separate tax-funded benefit that low income families had to apply to get through local social security offices. Many did not – initially about 30 per cent - though take-up gradually rose to over 80 per cent in the 1980s. Numbers on the benefit, and its successor, the Family Credit, rose from about 100,000 in 1973 to over half a million by the mid 1990s, mostly because family poverty grew.

The Labour government that followed kept FIS but introduced an extended version of the old Family Allowance called Child Benefit, which we still have. It was both more generous and went to the first child as well. It was paid for in large part by removing the tax advantages previously derived by taxpaying families and especially those paying tax at high levels from child tax allowances.

The same government tried to remedy the deficiencies of the flat rate state pension by introducing a wage related scheme on top, the State Earnings Related Pension Scheme (SERPS). This has since, indeed, topped up the pensions of many pensioners to raise them above the poverty line. But those in occupational schemes were always able to opt out. It never had time to become embedded in the political landscape and attract the powerful support enjoyed by the American, Swedish or German pension arrangements.

The other significant development of the 1970s was the recognition of the particular needs of those with disabilities and resulted from well organised groups and well articulated needs. Beveridge had largely ignored them except for those disabled at work or fighting in a war. The Attendance Allowance was introduced in 1972. A Mobility Allowance for those who found difficulty in getting about and who needed more costly forms of transport, an Invalid Care Allowance for those looking after those needing special attention, and other non-contributory benefits were introduced in 1976. They took some account of the extra costs disability caused. A given level of income might be above the poverty line for a fully mobile person but not for someone who needed more income to be equivalently mobile. This was an extension of the meaning and concept of poverty, as well as being important to those receiving the benefits. Numbers receiving Attendance Allowance rose from 145,000 to over 900,000 between 1973 and 1991. Numbers on Invalidity Benefit and Severe Disablement Allowance rose from 104,000 to 326,000 between 1973 and 1994. Numbers receiving Mobility Allowance rose from 62,000 in 1977 to nearly 700,000 in 1991 (Evans, 1998).

Women's poverty rediscovered

Another important feature of social science research begun in the 1970s and 1980s was the re-emergence of a feminist perspective on poverty. Poverty had its most profound impact on women and yet this was not seen or appreciated – 'Invisible Women, Invisible Poverty' as Jane Millar and Caroline Glendinning (1987) put it. Some of the insights were not new, as we saw earlier, but they were deepened and extended. New work was done on the distribution of income within the family and the importance of getting income to the mother (Pahl 1989). That was, in the end, to bear some fruit in the changes that were made to the tax credit schemes in the New Labour period. The work on the financial and other needs of carers which began in this period was mostly done by women (Parker, 1985; Glendinning, 1992). So, too, was the thorough and non-judgemental work on the change in families and single parenthood (Kiernan, Land and Lewis, 1998). Policy makers no longer have the excuse that these poverty situations are hidden.

Gathering clouds

The anti-poverty measures up to the mid 1970s do therefore have some kind of logical sequence. The needs of new poverty groups came to be articulated and pressed home. The scale and breadth of the safety net was gradually widened, even if its generosity was not. Social insurance remained the preferred social policy method for poverty avoidance, even if individuals in the top income groups had come increasingly to rely on occupation based forms of insurance against old age and short term sickness. It was the late 1970s and 1980s that brought the significant change both in the scale of the poverty problem and in the nature of the social policy response (Glennerster, 2000; Lowe, 1999).

6 The last quarter century
From New Right to New Labour

John Hills

It is tempting to try to divide periods of social policy and the evolution of their outcomes by neat political divisions – the election of the Conservative government of Margaret Thatcher in 1979, or of the 'New Labour' government of Tony Blair in 1997 being two of the most obvious discontinuities. However, events and policies do not necessarily change with such abrupt boundaries.

When the Thatcher Government came to power in 1979, income inequality and poverty were near to an all-time low. Two major policy directions of the new government were to restrain and reduce public spending – of which social security was a major part – and improve incentives to work.

For instance, one of the defining features of the Thatcher government was its aim of reducing public spending, particularly that on the 'welfare state'. But the post-war growth of social spending as a share of national income ended not in 1979, but in 1976, after the Labour cabinet minister Tony Crosland had announced that 'the party is over' and after the visit of the International Monetary Fund. And public spending restraint continued after May 1997, with New Labour fulfilling its election pledge to stick to Conservative spending plans for two years. By 1999/00, overall public spending (Total Managed Expenditure) had fallen to 37.4 per cent of GDP, fully two percentage points of national income below the lowest level achieved under the Conservatives (in 1988/89), and four points below the minimum under the Heath government of the early 1970s.

Similarly, perhaps the most important change in policy towards social security and poverty introduced by the Thatcher government was its decision in 1981 to adjust ('uprate') the value of social security benefits each year only in line with *price* inflation. For some key benefits, such as the basic state retirement pension, this broke with the previous policy of adjusting values in line with *earnings* growth. This makes it easier for the public finances to cope with benefit spending (as tax revenues tend to rise at least in line with incomes) but leaves those dependent on benefits further and further behind general living standards, and deeper in poverty (if a relative poverty line is used, as discussed in chapter 3 above). But New Labour has not reversed this decision as a default for most benefits. Instead, since 1999 it has been making selective increases in some benefits but not others, and devoting resources to reforms such as the new 'tax credits'. Many people have done better than they would have done under a policy of returning to earnings indexation without reform, but others have not and continue to live on incomes that are falling in relative terms.

In terms of outcomes, we have already seen in chapter 3 (figures 5 and 6) that relative poverty for the population as a whole reached a low point in the late 1970s. So did measures of the inequality of the income distribution. But depending on the exact measure chosen, the low point can be seen to be any of the years 1977, 1978 or 1979. The turning point in what some had come to see as Britain's steady progress towards becoming a more equal society did not necessarily coincide with the change of government, even if some of the Conservative government's policies would greatly accelerate that change.

This chapter therefore tries to take an overview of the last 25 years, looking across some of the themes which have been discussed in earlier chapters: overall policy towards poverty; public spending; the structure of social security; families and children; unemployment and incentives; and old age. It then looks at the outcomes of these policies and of other pressures on poverty rates.

Policy towards poverty

Poverty, inequality, and policies to reduce them, were not high on the Thatcher government's agenda. The Royal Commission on the Distribution of Income and Wealth established by Labour was wound up. The government tried hard (if unsuccessfully) to bury the report commissioned by Labour from Sir Douglas Black's committee on health inequalities and their links to poverty when it appeared in 1980. An interdepartmental Group on Poverty Study was tellingly renamed as the working group on Work Incentives and Income Compression (of which the author became a member), and its priorities for policy reform changed accordingly. Famously, in 1989 the then Social Security Secretary, John Moore, announced 'the end of the line for poverty', arguing that it was 'false and dangerous' to talk as if large parts of the British population were in dire need on the basis of poverty lines that rose with national prosperity (Timmins, 1995, pp. 450–1).

In one sense, the change in political priorities is understandable. Income inequality and poverty (whether measured in relative or absolute terms) *were* near to their all-time lows in 1979. Equally, economic growth and growth of average living standards had also been at post-war lows since the oil shocks of the early 1970s. The diagnosis of the incoming government was that the two were connected – via the disincentive effects of overgenerous social security benefits on the one hand, and by the effects on economic and productivity growth of an overlarge public sector on the other. Its policies were therefore aimed at restraining and reducing public spending – of which social security was a major part – and at changing the system to improve incentives to work. If challenged on the impact of such policies on the poor, the response echoed that of the parallel Reagan administration in the US in the 1980s – that the benefits of faster growth in living standards for those with high incomes allowed by lower taxes would 'trickle down' to those at the bottom.

There was little evidence of this happening in the 1980s. Instead, poverty and the response to it became dominated by four upward pressures. First, Britain went into deep economic recession in the early 1980s, followed by a brief boom in the second half of the decade, and then a renewed leap in unemployment at its end. Much of the subsequent evolution of social security can be seen as a response to this and its impact on public spending. Second, at the same time as the rise in unemployment and economic inactivity, the position of unskilled workers was weakening more generally in the labour market – the real value of the level of wages below which the bottom tenth of male earners fell was no higher in the early 1990s than it had been in the mid 1970s (Barclay, 1995, fig. 6). Third, society was changing. While 12 per cent of children were living in lone parent families in 1979, 20 per cent of children were by 1997. Such families were much more likely to be without an income from work and in poverty than others, and the 'breadwinner' based social insurance system bequeathed by Beveridge did little to help. Fourth, the country was ageing and the number of pensioners growing. While this was not in itself at such a dramatic rate, the cost of state pensions was set to

Minimum wage protesters in Brighton in 1995. Wages for the lowest paid were no higher in real terms in the early 1990s than they had been in the early 1970s.

grow rapidly as Barbara Castle's State Earnings Related Pension Scheme matured. Under its rules, full rights could accrue in 20 years, so someone with average earnings retiring in 1998 could receive an extra earnings-related pension from the state almost equalling in value what the basic pension had been in 1978. Although the rules were made less generous (for those retiring later) in 1988, proposals to abolish SERPS outright were rejected, and its cost grew.

All this left a contradiction in policy which has yet to be resolved. Attempting to restrain public spending growth in the face of such pressures, while avoiding outright cuts in benefits for the poorest, pushed governments particularly in the 1980s towards more reliance on the social safety net of what was Supplementary Benefit (and became Income Support) and on other forms of means testing. But this reliance increases the number of people affected by the disincentive effects of withdrawal of means tested benefit, contradicting the other overarching aim of policy of improving incentives.

Under John Major's government of the 1990s, policy became

less harsh. The regressive Poll Tax, used to finance local government through a flat rate charge on all adults, was abolished and replaced with the property related Council Tax. Crucially for the poorest, the right to an income related rebate of up to 100 per cent of the new tax's value was restored, whereas in theory everyone had been liable to pay at least 20 per cent of the Poll Tax, no matter how low their income. When tax rises came after the 1992 election, they bore more heavily on those with higher incomes. For a period in the mid 1990s, while average living standards rose only slowly, relative poverty fell slightly, and the growth in overall inequality halted.

Labour's election campaign in 1997 said and promised little about poverty. The manifesto contained just two references to poverty, one in the context of tax and benefit reform to reduce welfare dependency, and the other about helping people into jobs. It did promise to tackle educational disadvantage, to introduce a minimum wage, and to reduce long term unemployment, particularly among young people. One of the five 'early pledges' around which Labour built its campaign was to cut youth unemployment, using resources from a 'windfall tax' on the privatised utilities.

In office the first move was indeed the introduction of the 'New Deal' programmes designed to get people off benefits and into work. Shortly after the election the government announced a new Social Exclusion Unit , reporting directly to the Prime Minister, and focusing on problems of compounded disadvantage, particularly those that cut across Whitehall departments. At one point, Tony Blair described the unit as 'the defining difference' between New Labour and the Conservatives. However, in the autumn of 1997, New Labour found itself embroiled in a row around the abolition of special additional benefits for lone parents. This had been built into the Conservative spending plans to which Labour had committed itself, and the government pushed it through despite significant opposition from its own Members of Parliament. By the time of the March 1998 Budget it became clear that benefits and new tax credits were to be improved for all low income families in a way that meant few lone parents would actually lose out (indeed, they have been the largest gainers from New Labour's reforms). But by then many people's views of New Labour's priorities had been set and they would be slow to change.

In terms of policy presentation, the decisive moment came in March 1999, when Tony Blair used a lecture in memory of William Beveridge to announce: 'Our historic aim will be for ours to be the first generation to end child poverty. It is a 20-year mission, but I believe it can be done' (Blair, 1999). This was followed up by a specific target to cut child poverty in relative terms (against a benchmark of 60 per cent of current median income) by a quarter between 1998/99 and 2004/05. In 2004

In his Beveridge Lecture in 1999 Tony Blair pledged to eradicate child poverty within a generation.

that target was further extended to achieve a cut of a half by 2010/11, with the 20-year target now defined as being 'amongst the best in Europe' in terms of relative poverty – still very ambitious given Britain's starting point as the worst in Europe in the mid 1990s, with rates three to four times those in some Scandinavian countries.

In September 1999 the government also published its first annual report of progress on poverty and social exclusion, *Opportunity for All*. This outlined what the government saw as the key features driving poverty and exclusion: lack of opportunities to work or acquire education and skills; childhood deprivation; disrupted families; barriers to older people living active, fulfilling and healthy lives; inequalities in health; poor housing; poor neighbourhoods; fear of crime; and discrimination (DSS, 1999, p. 2).

Policy has followed along most of those dimensions, some of which are discussed in more detail below.[1] Promoting work and 'making work pay' has been prominent, involving not just the New Deals and the macroeconomic policies aimed to promote economic stability, but also the introduction of Britain's first National Minimum Wage, and the transformation of social security benefits into more generous tax credits. But at the same time, and in contrast to policies in the US, allowances for the children of those who are out of work have also been increased well above inflation. After dropping to a low point in 1999, public spending on education is rising, with particular emphasis on poorly performing schools. Policy towards pensioners has been selective, focused on increasing the value of the means tested minimum (now known as the 'guarantee credit' of the Pension Credit). The universal basic pension has remained linked to prices in most years, although all pensioners have benefited from various other measures, such as an annual 'winter fuel allowance'. At the 2002 Labour Party Conference Gordon Brown pledged that 'Our aim is to end pensioner poverty in our country', although unlike the child poverty commitment there is no timescale or specific benchmark for this.

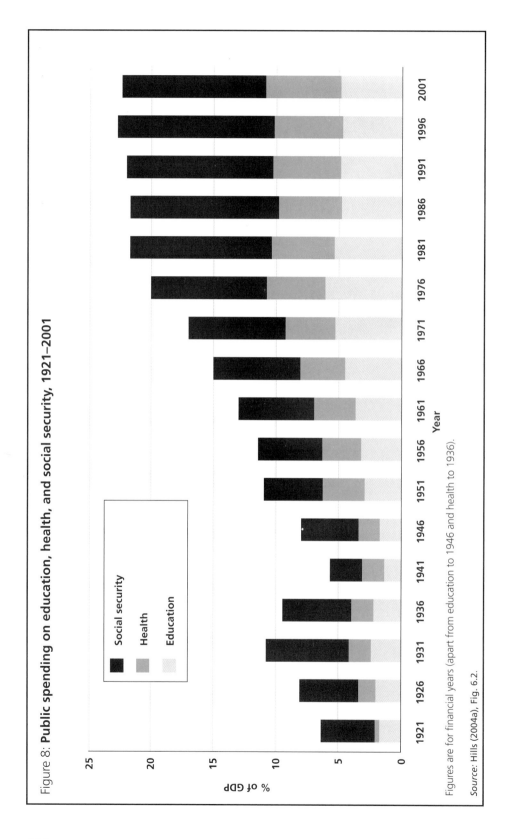

Figure 8: **Public spending on education, health, and social security, 1921–2001**

Figures are for financial years (apart from education to 1946 and health to 1936).

Source: Hills (2004a), Fig. 6.2.

An accumulation of evidence had shown the ways in which the country had become more polarised between different kinds of area, not just as the old industrial regions declined, but also within towns and cities across the country (Hills, 1995). The biggest part of the Social Exclusion Unit's work led to the establishment of a National Strategy for Neighbourhood Renewal and to New Labour's most ambitious target, that 'within 10–20 years, no one should be seriously disadvantaged by where they live'. A set of 'floor targets' has been set for achievement in employment, education, crime, health and housing in the most disadvantaged areas. Some of the related policies have been for 'mainstream services', such as health, education and policing, but others have been targeted on particular areas, such as the New Deal for Communities, neighbourhood wardens, the Sure Start early years programmes, and Excellence in Cities for education.[2]

Unlike the US in the early 1960s, there has been no declaration of 'War on Poverty', and nor is there any overarching target to reduce poverty overall, as there is in Ireland. But none the less, by the start of the twenty-first century there was a commitment to tackle poverty and disadvantage that had not been seen since the 1960s, if not the 1940s, and a raft of specific policy initiatives aimed at particular aspects of the problem. The issue for the future is whether the scope of these is enough, and what could be done to fill the gaps in them (see chapter 7).

Public spending

Although governments can affect income distribution and poverty in other ways, the largest effects come from the combination of public spending and the taxes that pay for it. This is not just a matter of spending on social security benefits, but also that on other elements of what is sometimes called the 'social wage' – health care, education, housing, and personal social services (Sefton, 2002).

As figure 8 shows, the total of the three largest elements of

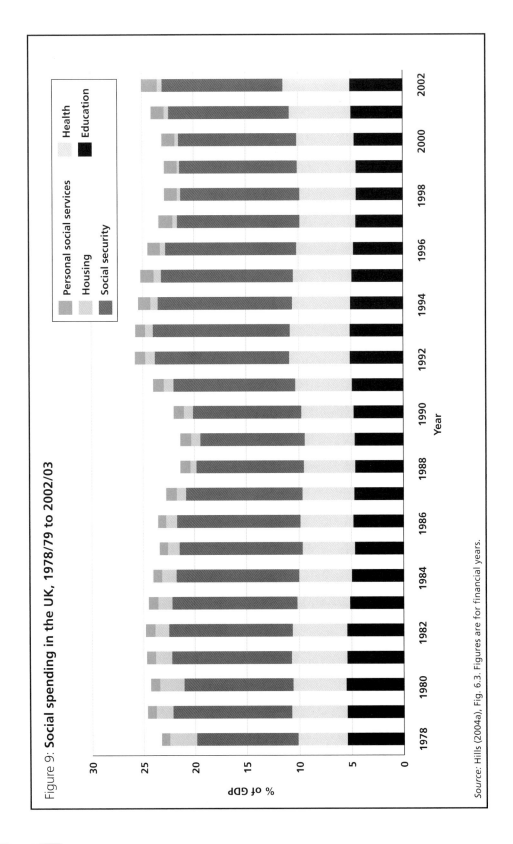

Figure 9: **Social spending in the UK, 1978/79 to 2002/03**

Source: Hills (2004a), Fig. 6.3. Figures are for financial years.

social spending, health, education and social security, had reached 10 per cent of national income in the 1930s. Its main period of growth came in the 30 years after the end of the Second World War, taking the total to 20 per cent of national income by 1976/77.

Since then social spending more widely defined has fluctuated around a quarter of national income – indeed, equalling this in both 1979/80, the Thatcher government's first year in office, and in 2002/03, New Labour's sixth year (figure 9). A large part of the variation in the last quarter century has related to the state of the economy, with social security spending rising in the recessions of the early 1980s and early 1990s, and falling again in the subsequent recoveries. More recently, policy changes have had a clearer effect – the post-1997 election austerity leading to the low point of social spending in 1999/00, and subsequent policies that have increased spending, notably taking the total of health and education spending to their highest share of GDP ever by the end of the period shown. In contrast, housing spending has become a much smaller share of the total over the 25 years, and social security (even including the new tax credits) is a smaller share of GDP than ten years ago.

The comparatively static total results from the collision of two opposing forces: the desire to reduce public spending to allow lower taxes, particularly in the 1980s; and the upward pressures on pensions, social services and health care from an ageing population, on social security from higher levels of market inequality, and on almost all of these items from growing affluence. As we get richer, many of the items social spending covers – notably health care and education – are ones to which we want to devote an increasing proportion of income. As we discuss in the next chapter, these pressures are unlikely to get any easier. Over much of the last 25 years, policies 'put the lid' on social spending, but did so at a cost of growing means testing, falling relative incomes for the poorest, and tight constriction of public services in relation to public

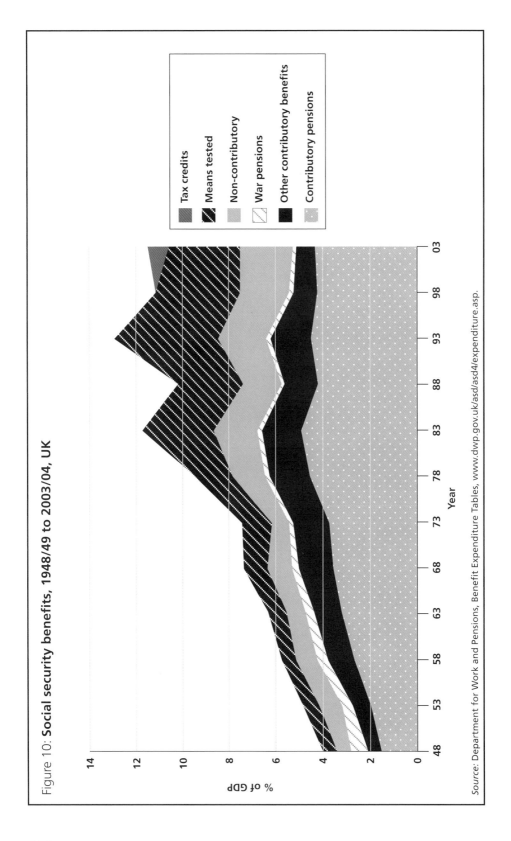

Figure 10: **Social security benefits, 1948/49 to 2003/04, UK**

Source: Department for Work and Pensions, Benefit Expenditure Tables, www.dwp.gov.uk/asd/asd4/expenditure.asp.

demands for them. More recently some growth in social spending has been accommodated without a large increase in taxes as a share of GDP through squeezing down other parts of public spending (notably defence and debt interest). However, the room to do this is narrowing, leaving policy makers with some increasingly uncomfortable choices (Hills, 2004a, ch. 11).

The structure of social security

As the previous chapter described, the reforms of the Attlee government in the 1940s, following the Beveridge Report, attempted to make the National Insurance system the major part of social security, with minimal reliance on means tested benefits. As discussed, this did not happen, partly because new risks emerged which were not covered well by the 'breadwinner' based Beveridge model (Baldwin and Falkingham, 1994), but also because contributory social insurance benefits were never set at a high enough level to get recipients clear of the acceptable minimum, particularly after allowing for housing costs. None the less, led by spending on the basic pension, contributory benefits did dominate the social security budget for more than 30 years, representing three-quarters of all benefits in 1973/74, and reaching a peak of 6.5 per cent of national income ten years later (figure 10).

But for 30 years now, despite the introduction of the contribution based State Earnings Related Pension Scheme in 1978, the role of insurance benefits within the system has been in retreat. The large increases in social security spending in the early 1980s and early 1990s took the form of means tested benefits. At the same time, the role of non-means tested, but also non-contributory, benefits (such as Child Benefit or some disability benefits) has also increased. Two pressures have rolled back the role of National Insurance. First, under Conservative governments in the early 1970s and the 1980s, the emphasis was on trying to 'target' a constrained budget most efficiently, with means testing seen as the way to do this. As far as pensions are concerned, this process has continued since 1997.

Conditions for receiving insurance benefits were also tightened, and their generosity reduced, particularly with the removal of earnings related additions to unemployment and sickness benefits in the 1980s.

At other times, however, it has been the restrictive nature of contribution conditions – particularly for those with a limited work record – that has led governments with more inclusive aims to increase the emphasis on non-contributory benefits. Together, these pressures from both left and right have led to the steady decline of the contributory system. The roots of this were discussed in chapter 5: an important factor was that, unlike many other European countries, the UK had a comprehensive – and fairly effective – means tested minimum to fall back on as social insurance came under pressure. The very strength of the safety net made the rundown of social insurance possible both politically and administratively in a way that it would not have been elsewhere.

More recently, since 1998 some of what were social security benefits – the old Family Credit (originally Family Income Supplement) and Income Support allowances for children – have been transformed into 'tax credits'. The distributional effects of this are discussed below, but one aim of the exercise has been to destigmatise payments, making them part of the tax machinery and associating them with the government's 'making work pay' rhetoric. Whether this has improved take-up – a besetting problem with means tested benefits – is still unclear, but it has certainly allowed extra resources to go in this direction (some of them outside what would otherwise have been called 'public spending') in way that might otherwise have been politically more difficult.

The other crucial change of the last quarter century has been the change in the values of benefits, both relative to each other, and relative to other incomes. Different parts of the benefit system have been treated in different ways. Figure 11 shows what has happened since 1971 to the values of four example benefits: the single basic state retirement pension;

Income Support (or its equivalent) for single pensioners; unemployment benefit (now Jobseeker's Allowance or JSA) for single people; and Income Support for single people aged 25 to 60. The first panel shows their values in real terms, the second one values relative to average adult earnings.[3] The basic pension increased significantly in real terms between 1971 and 1983, after which the early 1980s policy decision of the Thatcher government to link most benefit levels to prices rather than to earnings or other incomes took effect, and its real value stayed much the same until the end of the 1990s. In some recent years its real value has increased under New Labour following a commitment to a minimum cash increase each year (reacting to the political furore when low inflation led to a cash increase of only 75p per week one year). The basic policy remains one of protecting only its real value, however. As a result, the second panel shows that its relative value fell from 26 per cent of average earnings in 1983 to 18 per cent by 1990, and 16 per cent by 2002. By contrast, the real value of Income Support for pensioners has increased steadily since 1976, including through the 1980s, but with particularly large increases since 1998. As a result, the value of the means tested minimum for a single pensioner was almost as great in relation to average earnings in 2002 as it had been in 1971.

The decline in the relative value of unemployment benefit since its link with the pension was broken in 1973 has been even greater, particularly since the early 1980s, falling from 21 per cent of average earnings in 1979 to 12 per cent by 2002. In this case the values of non-means tested and means tested benefits had converged by the end of the period. As the figure shows, social security benefits for working age people *without* children have continued to fall in relative value since 1997.

Families and children

One of the main social security reforms of the late 1970s had been the amalgamation of the old family allowances with income tax child allowances. The former, also stemming from

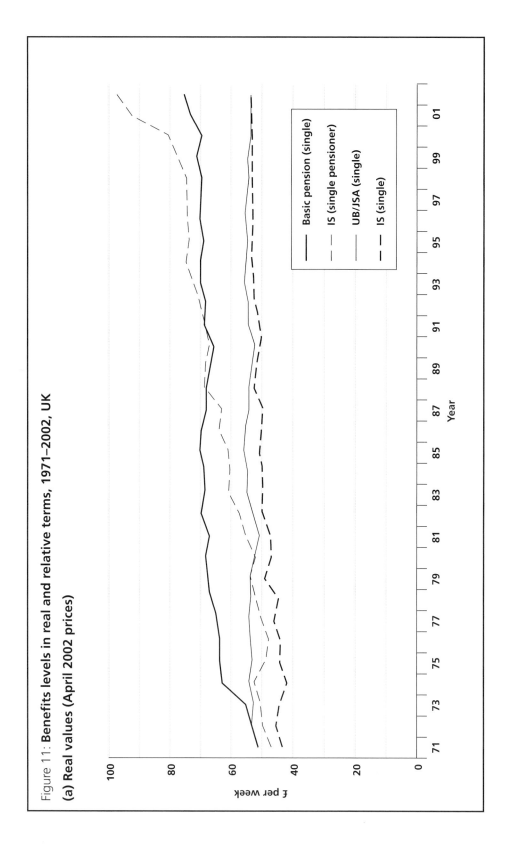

Figure 11: Benefits levels in real and relative terms, 1971–2002, UK

(a) Real values (April 2002 prices)

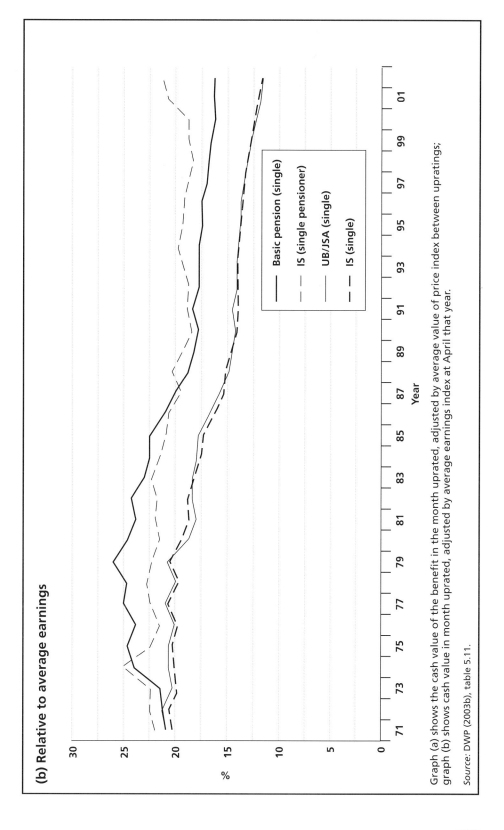

(b) Relative to average earnings

Legend:
- Basic pension (single)
- IS (single pensioner)
- UB/JSA (single)
- IS (single)

Year

%

Graph (a) shows the cash value of the benefit in the month uprated, adjusted by average value of price index between upratings; graph (b) shows cash value in month uprated, adjusted by average earnings index at April that year.

Source: DWP (2003b), table 5.11.

the 1940s, had not been paid for the first child. The latter had delivered nothing to non-taxpayers, the poorest, and most to those paying the highest rates of income tax. By contrast, the new Child Benefit was paid equally in respect of all children. This has great advantages in achieving almost complete take-up, and in avoiding the disincentives associated with means tested alternatives. Its proponents – notably the Child Poverty Action Group under its then director, Frank Field – had pointed in the 1970s to its universal nature as a source of political strength: the 'sharp elbows of the middle classes' would resist attempts to cut it back, and so protect poor families at the same time. This very feature, however, made Child Benefit the focus of attention when the government was trying to cut back public spending in the 1980s – why should scarce public resources go to the middle classes, even, as was often pointed out, to the Duchess of Westminster, wife of the richest man in the country?

The end result of such pressure was a three year period when the cash value of Child Benefit was frozen in the late 1980s, while under the 'Fowler reforms' of 1988 the means tested benefit for families with children and low earnings was renamed Family Credit and made more generous. The 'sharp elbows' had their effect under the Major government, however, and Child Benefit was unfrozen and increased for the first child.

An innovation of the early 1990s was the introduction of the Child Support Agency from 1993 in response to the growing numbers of lone parents, high poverty levels among lone parent families, and the extent to which such families were reliant on social security benefits, particularly Income Support. The aim of the CSA is to try to improve the very low levels of maintenance paid by 'absent parents' (usually fathers) to 'parents with care' (usually mothers). In trying to do this it faces difficulties both in assessing how much absent parents (often part of a new family with children) can afford to pay, and in enforcing payment. The second difficulty is compounded when the parent with care is receiving Income Support and little or no

Table 9: **Increases in Child Benefit, Income Support and net income after housing costs, April 1991 to April 2003 (£ per week, April 2003 prices)**

	April 1991	April 1997	April 2003	Change 1991–1997 (%)	Change 1997–2003 (%)
Child Benefit (first child)	11.23	12.81	16.05	14.1	25.3
Child Benefit (subsequent children)	9.87	10.43	10.75	5.7	3.1
Income Support (lone parent, 1 child under 11)	87.70	91.18	108.90	4.0	19.4
Income Support (couple, 1 child under 11)	112.03	116.87	140.00	4.3	19.8
Income Support (couple, 2 children under 11)	129.93	135.71	178.50	4.4	31.5
Net income after housing costs					
Couple, 2 children, on average earnings	297.18	311.73	352.00	4.9	12.9
Lone parent, 1 child, on average earnings	217.64	229.33	266.22	5.4	16.1
Couple, 2 children, on half average earnings	165.13	177.61	239.90	7.6	35.1
Lone parent, 1 child, on half average earnings	146.01	156.95	193.55	7.5	23.3

Source: Stewart (2005a), based on DWP (2004).

benefit from child support payments ends up with them, resulting instead in a saving to government in the Income Support which has to be paid.

It is in the tax and benefit treatment of families with children that New Labour has made its largest changes, as the figures for the values of benefits and tax credits in table 9 show. Child Benefit paid for the first child had increased by 14 per cent in real terms between 1991 and 1997, but Income Support levels for families had changed little in real terms. Nor had there been much rise in the real incomes (after housing costs) of families with children on average or below average earnings, allowing for the tax system and benefits they could have received. Over the following six years, the picture was very different. Child Benefit for the first child increased by a quarter in real terms,[4] and Income Support for families with young children rose by at least a fifth (more for larger families). The real value of the child element for a child aged under 11 (£27.75 per week) of the new Child Tax Credit when it was introduced in April 2003 was twice as high as its equivalent under the old Family Credit system had been in 1997 (Hills, 2004a, table 9.1). As a result of this and other tax and tax credit changes, a couple with two children and wages of half average earnings were a third better off in real terms in 2003 than they had been in 1997.

This has been a major commitment by the government. Between 1997/98 and 2002/03, spending on child-contingent benefits rose from 1.38 to 2.04 per cent of GDP. Spending on early years policies and child care grew from 0.21 to 0.33 per cent of GDP (Stewart, 2005a, table 7.9). Even before the reforms associated with Child Tax Credit in April 2003, the additional commitment to cash and services for children represented 0.8 per cent of GDP. By 2004, the additional spending had reached 1 per cent of national income.

The unemployed and incentives to work

Although benefits for those classed as unemployed make up only a very small part of the social security budget (5 per cent in 2001/02), their structure and the disincentives they may create have continued to be a major focus of attention in the last quarter century. This is not least because they are generally believed to be such a large part of the budget: 44 per cent of respondents to the 2001 British Social Attitudes survey thought that they were the largest item in social security spending, and a further 27 per cent thought them the next largest part (Taylor-Gooby and Hastie, 2002). Large proportions of the population believe that the benefits make unemployed people less likely to look for work and that the system is widely abused through fraud (Hills, 2004a, figs 6.11 and 6.13).

This was certainly the belief of the Thatcher government when it came into power, leading it to set in place a series of measures that reduced benefit entitlements, particularly to national insurance based Unemployment Benefit (now known as insurance based Jobseeker's Allowance). The aim was to reduce 'replacement rates', the ratio between incomes out of work and those in work. As well as adjusting the values of benefits in line only with prices each year (with the effects on values relative to earnings shown in figure 11 above), additions related to previous earnings were abolished, conditions related to previous contributions made tighter, and the lengths of entitlement to non-means tested benefits were cut. In all, Atkinson and Micklewright (1989) recorded 38 changes to the system of benefits for the unemployed in the 1980s, nearly all of them reducing entitlements.

Despite this, the numbers unemployed remained high. One effect of the changes was to increase the numbers receiving means tested Income Support. At the same time, tacit encouragement was given by the government for people to be recorded as out of work due to invalidity (now 'incapacity') rather than to be looking for work. As old heavy industries were 'shaken out', the number of people – particularly older men – who were of working age but economically inactive grew rapidly, particularly in the old industrial parts of the country. Economic inactivity for working age men grew from 12 per cent in the late 1980s to 15 per cent by 1997, and continued to grow slowly, reaching 16 per cent by 2003 (McKnight, 2005, fig. 2.3).

Over time, however, the emphasis on 'active labour market measures' – assistance and encouragement with job search and training – rather than on reducing incomes out of work gradually increased. This eventually led to the introduction of Jobseeker's Allowance in 1996. Entitlement to non-means tested benefit was again cut, this time to six months, but the emphasis on support for job-search and training was increased.

In many ways, New Labour's 'New Deal' programmes can be seen as a continuation of the direction already taken by the Major government's JSA reforms – but with considerably more resources put into positive supports, particularly for the young unemployed.

Evaluations of most of these active labour market – or 'welfare to work' – programmes consistently show positive but small effects (McKnight, 2005). For instance, a recent evaluation of New Labour's flagship New Deal for Young People suggests that it has been a success, and represents good value for money – but that there are only 17,000 extra young people in work as a result of it than there would otherwise have been (Van Reenan, 2004). Such effects are useful, and almost certainly crucial in winning public backing for overall support for unemployed people, but by themselves hardly transform the picture.

At the same time, the incentive effects of all of these reforms have been ambiguous. In the Conservative period, incomes for those out of work were reduced by comparison with incomes in work. However, the effects of this were sometimes blunted – both by the increasing incidence of low pay and by factors such as Housing Benefit. As housing subsidies were reduced, and rents rose, the availability of benefit covering 100 per cent of rent for those with the lowest incomes became a larger part of the equation. Faced with rapidly rising costs of Housing Benefit, but still trying to preserve the integrity of the national minimum, assistance for those just above the minimum was cut back. The 'tapers' in both Housing Benefit and Council Tax Benefit became steeper, leaving little gain from extra earnings for those affected by them.

This contributed to further deepening the 'poverty trap', the phenomenon first identified in the 1960s that the combination of taxes on additional income and withdrawal of means tested benefits could mean that poor families would need very large increases in gross earnings for there to be any noticeable effect on raising their net income. Figure 12 shows the end result of

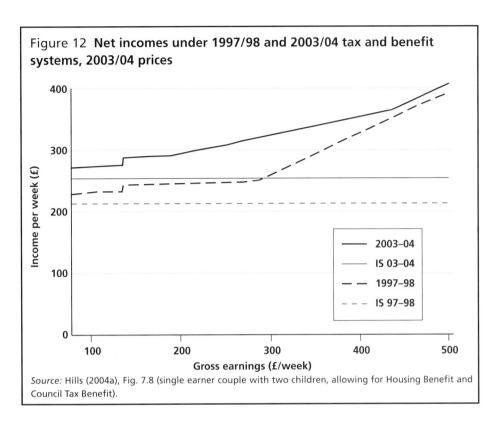

Figure 12 **Net incomes under 1997/98 and 2003/04 tax and benefit systems, 2003/04 prices**

Source: Hills (2004a), Fig. 7.8 (single earner couple with two children, allowing for Housing Benefit and Council Tax Benefit).

the Conservative reforms, giving the position in 1997/98 (adjusted to 2003/04 prices) of a one earner couple with two children, who were also tenants. As can be seen, over a considerable range of gross income, net income would hardly have risen at all even if earnings rose substantially. With gross earnings of £75 per week, their net income would have been £227. With gross earnings of £275, net income would only have risen to £248: a £200 increase in earnings would have left them only £21 better off (before allowing for any resultant increased costs of working such as transport or child care). As a result, even with earnings of £275 per week, the difference between net income in work and that out of work (on Income Support of £211 at 2003/04 prices, including help with housing costs) remained small.

New Labour's reforms, culminating in the introduction of the Child Tax Credit and Working Tax Credit in April 2003, have changed the position in three ways. First, incomes out of work and on Income Support have been increased. At the very lowest levels of earnings, the gain from working remains low. But figure 12 shows that for those with somewhat higher earnings the system has been made much more generous – there is both a larger gain from earning more, and for earnings above about £250 per week there is a much larger margin over income out of work. However, the third effect is that the way in which higher earnings lead to reduced tax credits now extends over a much wider income range – in this case up to earnings of £420 per week. The poverty trap has been made shallower but wider.

Figure 13 shows this effect in another way. In this case it shows the 'effective marginal tax rates' facing the families in figure 12 in the 1997/98 and 2003/04 systems: what percentage of any increase in gross income would be lost through income tax, National Insurance contributions, benefit and tax credit withdrawal. In the 1997/98 system, rates were near to 100 per cent right up to earnings of £275 per week. In the 2003/04 system, this range is much shorter, ending at £200 per week. But the cost of this is that the family faces a 70 per cent effective marginal tax rate over a much wider range.[5]

The Treasury calculates that under the 1997/98 system 740,000 working families faced effective marginal tax rates *above* 70 per cent, and that only 270,000 do so in the 2004/05 system (HM Treasury, 2003b, table 4.2). However, 1.8 million now face rates 'above 60 per cent' (mostly actually facing 70 per cent exactly), compared with only 760,000 before. Acute disincentives affecting a smaller number have been replaced with less acute ones facing many more. So far the evidence is that on balance the reforms – despite their greater generosity to families who have children and who are out of work or on low wages – have had a net *positive* effect on labour supply (Brewer et al., 2003). A problem facing future policy is, however, that any extension of generosity of the tax credit system to help further reduce poverty also means extending the problem to higher income ranges (or increasing tax credit withdrawal rates, so deepening the poverty trap again). The

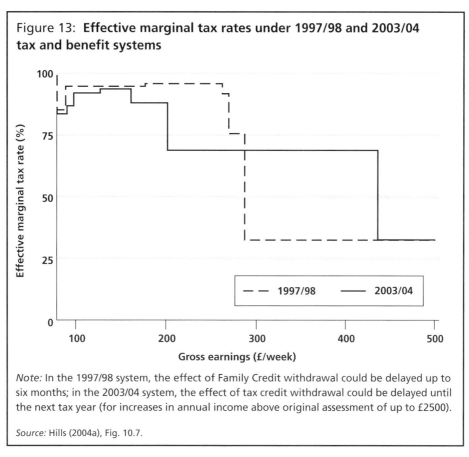

Figure 13: **Effective marginal tax rates under 1997/98 and 2003/04 tax and benefit systems**

Note: In the 1997/98 system, the effect of Family Credit withdrawal could be delayed up to six months; in the 2003/04 system, the effect of tax credit withdrawal could be delayed until the next tax year (for increases in annual income above original assessment of up to £2500).

Source: Hills (2004a), Fig. 10.7.

effect can be compounded by other means tests – for instance within student support or Education Maintenance Allowances for young people staying on in education after 16.

Pensions

The main changes to pensions policy in the last 25 years have already been touched on above. Perhaps strangely, the overall effect has been that policy has gone full circle. In a very convoluted way, current plans for future pensions are designed to return state support for pensioners to something not so distant from Beveridge's model of equal support for all (Hills, 2004b).

The first reform was set in motion in the 1970s – Barbara Castle's State Earnings Related Pension Scheme (SERPS) started in 1978. The principle of this was that as well as entitlement to the flat rate basic state pension (worth nearly a quarter of average earnings in 1978), people would also build up rights which related to the earnings on which they paid National Insurance contributions – worth a quarter of their own average lifetime earnings (in excess of each year's lower limit). This would get those with reasonable earnings well clear of the poverty line in retirement, even if they were not members of a private pension scheme.

However, the incoming Conservative government was not prepared to accept the additional cost of state pensions as a share of GDP that this would imply if the relative value of the basic pension was also to be maintained. In effect, the decision to cut the link between the value of the basic pension and earnings growth (with the effects shown in figure 11) created the fiscal headroom to pay for the growing costs of SERPS over the 1980s and 1990s. Instead of Barbara Castle's vision of the new system leading to gains for all pensioners, the end result has been lower pensions for those with low lifetime earnings, and higher ones for those who were better off at work.

For the future, the Fowler reforms of 1988 cut back the rate at which SERPS rights would accrue, and policy continued through the 1990s and past 1997 on the assumption that the value of the basic pension would continue to fall in relative terms – until it eventually became 'nugatory', in Michael Portillo's famous description of it in 1993.

New Labour has not reversed this, but instead has changed the system in three ways designed to redress the regressive impact of the policy changes of the previous 20 years:

- First, it has increased the value of the means tested minimum significantly, as figure 11 shows, renaming it first as the Minimum Income Guarantee, and then as the guarantee credit of the Pension Credit. The assumption of current policy is that the value of this will continue to rise with earnings growth (while the basic pension remains price linked).
- Second, from October 2003 it extended means tested support

through the Pension Credit to pensioners with small incomes that put them just above the means tested minimum. As with the reforms for working families illustrated above, the effect of this is to reduce the sharpest part of means testing, but to extend a milder form of it over a wider range of income. If indexation continues as in recent years, the scope of Pension Credit will steadily widen. Some estimates suggest that over 60 per cent of pensioners would eventually be affected by Pension Credit withdrawal.

- Third, it has changed the rules of SERPS – renaming it as the State Second Pension (S2P) – to increase its value for low earners. This will over time make its value considerably less earnings related and more flat rate than SERPS.

These reforms interact in a complicated way, and one that will change over time. Figure 14 gives one impact of the long run effect if current indexation rules continue. This shows state support on retirement in 1978, 1998 and projected for 2038, for a simple case of a single person whose earnings had (unrealistically) equalled the same proportion of the national average through his or her working life.[6]

- The solid line shows the position for someone retiring back in 1978, before SERPS was introduced. Both the basic pension and the minimum income guaranteed by what was then Supplementary Benefit were around 25 per cent of average earnings, so state support was virtually flat rate.
- The lighter dashed line shows the position for those retiring in 1998, when earnings related rights through SERPS were at their highest, but both Income Support and the basic state pension had fallen in relation to average earnings. State support had fallen for low earners, but had risen for higher earners.[7]
- The heavier dashed line shows a projection of state support in 2038 if current indexation policies continue. The minimum level of state support would, as now, be higher than in 1998

in relation to earnings (figure 11). For those with lifetime earnings below three quarters of the adult average, the level of support would also be higher than in 1998 as a result of the combined State Second Pension and Pension Credit reforms. However, for average and above average earners, entitlements would be lower (reflecting a considerable fall in the basic pension in relation to average earnings, as well as slower accrual of rights to the State Second Pension).[8]

What perhaps stands out from the diagram is the extent to which the effect of the reforms of the last few years has been to unwind the earnings related pensions introduced by Labour (and associated with Barbara Castle) in the late 1970s, eventually returning the support given by the system to something not so far from the original flat rate system of 1978 (itself dating from the reforms of the Attlee government in 1948). The emerging system does this in a far more complex way, however, with much more reliance on means testing.

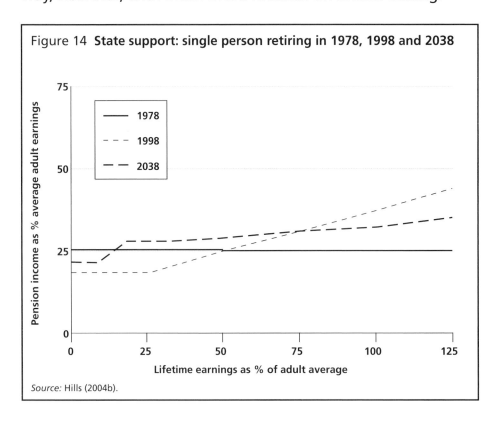

Figure 14 **State support: single person retiring in 1978, 1998 and 2038**

Source: Hills (2004b).

Outcomes

The combination of the impact of these social policy changes and the macroeconomic story of the last quarter century has led to contrasting fortunes for different parts of the income distribution and kinds of family. Figure 15, based on analysis by the Institute for Fiscal Studies, contrasts what has happened to the annual growth rates of net incomes (adjusted for family size) of those in successive fifths of the income distribution under the last three prime ministers (up to 2002/03 for Tony Blair).

While Mrs Thatcher was Prime Minister, incomes at the top grew rapidly. Lower down the distribution they grew much less fast, and at the bottom by very little. Average living standards grew, but income inequality widened rapidly, and the poor fell behind. During the Major years, the growth in inequality was partly reversed, but there was only slow growth in living standards for any of the groups. After 1997, all income groups enjoyed quite rapid growth in living standards. This has only meant a slow decline in *relative* poverty, but it did involve much faster growth in living standards for the poor than either of the earlier periods, and so resulted in rapid falls in *absolute* poverty. For many concerned with disadvantage, the latest period is clearly preferable to the other two, even though it has not resulted in a fall in inequality between the incomes of the top and the bottom. Indeed, inequality between the very top and the very bottom was still greater in 2002/03 than it had been in 1996/97. It was, however, falling if measured between those *near* the top and those *near* the bottom (Sefton and Sutherland, 2005).

Figure 16 gives a more detailed view of the changes in relative poverty over the last 40 years that we previously showed in figure 5, showing the composition of the population with incomes below half the contemporary average. Key features include:

• Overall relative poverty, which had been about 10 per cent of

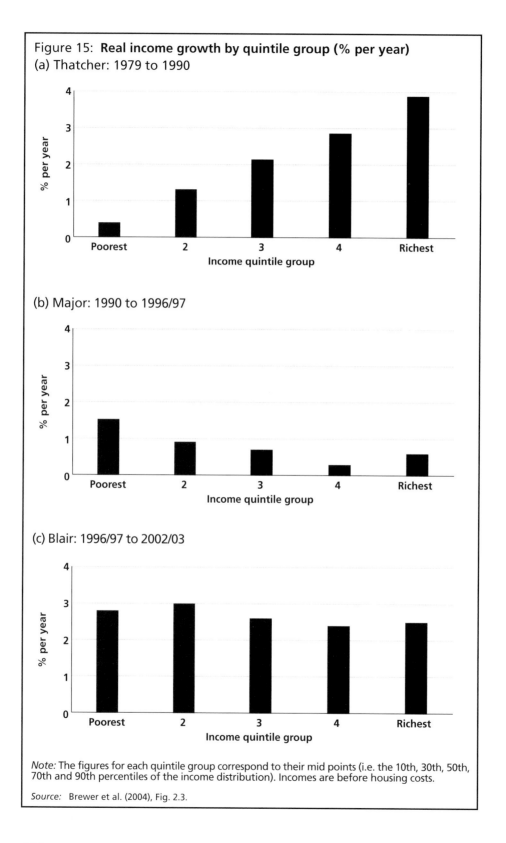

Figure 15: **Real income growth by quintile group (% per year)**
(a) Thatcher: 1979 to 1990

(b) Major: 1990 to 1996/97

(c) Blair: 1996/97 to 2002/03

Note: The figures for each quintile group correspond to their mid points (i.e. the 10th, 30th, 50th, 70th and 90th percentiles of the income distribution). Incomes are before housing costs.

Source: Brewer et al. (2004), Fig. 2.3.

the population in the 1960s, dipped to a low point of 6 per cent in 1977, but then grew very rapidly through the 1980s to peak at 21 per cent in the early 1990s. After a dip and then rise back in the mid 1990s it has fallen slowly since 1996/97. It is still three times its level of the mid 1970s.

- Pensioners made up a much greater proportion of the poor population in the 1960s than they do now. None the less, poor pensioners now represent as great a proportion of the whole population – nearly 5 per cent – as they did then.
- Families with children have become a much greater part of the poor population, not just lone parents and their children, but also two parent families. Most recently, their poverty rates have been falling.
- By contrast, there has been no recent fall in poverty rates for working age single people and couples *without* children.

Table 10 illustrates this last point in a little more detail for the period since 1979, in this case using poverty lines based on the current official measure of 60 per cent of median income. It shows poverty rates both in relative terms in the upper panel and against a fixed real line in the lower panel. For the 1996/97 to 2002/03 period, it shows how the slight fall in poverty rates for people of working age has resulted from a fall in poverty for those with children – falling child poverty has to involve falling *parent* poverty – but a *rise* in poverty for working age adults without children. While some of this group have benefited from New Labour's welfare-to-work programmes and the buoyant economy, others still dependent on benefits have had living standards which have fallen in relative terms.

The lower panel of the table gives a measure, however, of just how hard it is to achieve reductions against the moving target of a relative poverty standard when overall living standards are rising as fast as those shown in figure 15. Instead, it shows poverty rates against a fixed real standard – of the kind, for instance, used to measure official poverty rates in the US. Fewer people were poor in 1996/97 against this fixed line

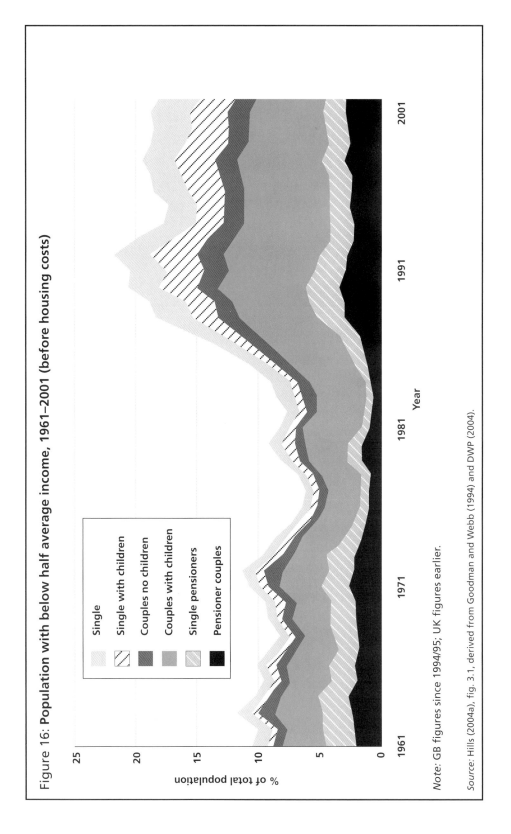

Figure 16: **Population with below half average income, 1961–2001 (before housing costs)**

Legend:
- Single
- Single with children
- Couples no children
- Couples with children
- Single pensioners
- Pensioner couples

Note: GB figures since 1994/95; UK figures earlier.

Source: Hills (2004a), fig. 3.1, derived from Goodman and Webb (1994) and DWP (2004).

Table 10: **Trends in poverty against relative and absolute income thresholds**

	1979	1996/97[1]	2002/03
Relative poverty: income below 60% of contemporary median (%):			
All	12	18	17
Children	12	25	21
Pensioners	28	21	21
Working age adults	7	15	14
of which those with children	n/a	19	16
of which those without children	n/a	12	13
Absolute poverty: income below 60% of 1996/97 median in real terms (%):			
All	30	18	10
Children	34	25	12
Pensioners	62	21	12
Working age adults	19	15	10
of which those with children	n/a	19	10
of which those without children	n/a	12	9

Note: Based on net equivalised household incomes before housing costs.
1 1996/97 is financial year. These and later figures are for GB (earlier figures are for UK).
Source: Sefton and Sutherland (2005), based on DWP (2004).

than had been in 1979. The fall was particularly large for pensioners, but much less for children, despite the increase of more than 40 per cent in average real incomes. In the period since 1996/97, the rate of fall has been faster. Indeed, child poverty against this kind of standard more than halved in just six years.

These figures are the most recent available at the time of writing, but do not take into account some of the largest changes that have been made by New Labour, those associated with the introduction of the Child and Working Tax Credits in April 2003 (replacing the Working Families Tax Credit – successor to Family Credit – and the child allowances previously in Income Support), and of the Pension Credit in October 2003.

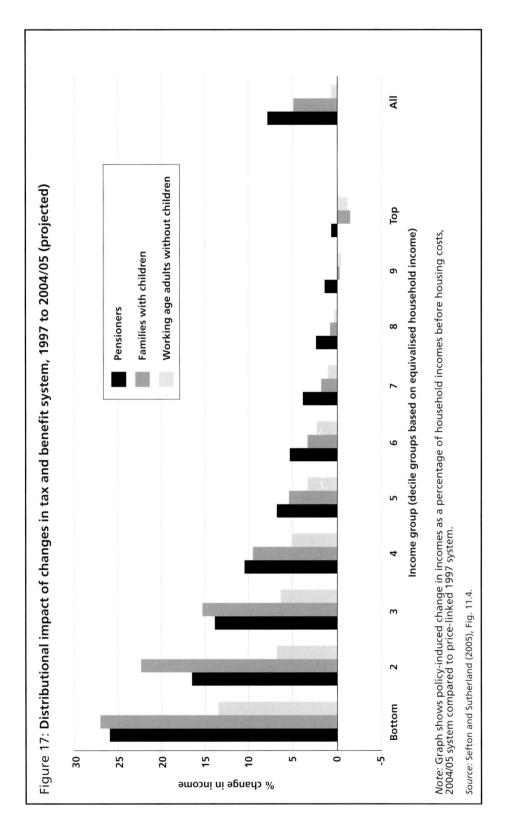

Figure 17: Distributional impact of changes in tax and benefit system, 1997 to 2004/05 (projected)

Note: Graph shows policy-induced change in incomes as a percentage of household incomes before housing costs, 2004/05 system compared to price-linked 1997 system.

Source: Sefton and Sutherland (2005), Fig. 11.4.

Modelling work suggests that these changes will add to the redistributive effects of the reforms. Figure 17 shows the results of one such exercise. It shows the effect on the incomes of successive tenths of the income distribution if one compares the actual 2004/05 tax and benefit system with the system that would have been in place if the 1997 system had been retained, simply uprated for price inflation.

Two things are clear from this. First, the reforms overall have been progressive, with the largest proportionate gains for the lower income groups. Second, it is pensioners and families with children that have been the largest gainers – gains equivalent to a quarter or more of income for those in the poorest tenth. On average, there has been little effect on people of working age without children, although even here there have been gains for some with low incomes (reflecting some reforms such as the National Minimum Wage and changes to National Insurance contributions as well as the Working Tax Credit, which now goes to some without children). Using this modelling, Sefton and Sutherland (2005, table 11.5) project that, other things being equal, the poverty rates shown in table 10 would fall further by 2004/05 to 15 per cent for children, 19 per cent for pensioners (each from 21 per cent in 2002/03), but would remain at 13 per cent for working age people without children. This would mean that the government would hit (on this basis, measuring incomes before deducting housing costs) its target for cutting child poverty by a quarter.

There is one caveat to this way of measuring the impact of policy on poverty. This is that the base used in figure 17 is that of the 1997 system adjusted only for price inflation. It could be argued that this gives an unduly positive impression of the impact of New Labour's policies at the bottom. After all, the comparison being made is with a world where (price linked) benefit rates would be falling behind other living standards, and so relative poverty rates would be *rising*. At the same time, tax revenues would be rising faster than national income, as 'fiscal drag' pulled more people into the tax net and into higher tax rates. This would not be a 'steady state' – the public finances would be continually improving while the poor were left behind.

As an alternative, the actual system can be compared with what it would have looked like if the 1997 tax and benefit system had been adjusted by *earnings* growth – in other words one where an 'Old Labour' policy of uprating benefits in line with earnings had been followed, but without any reform. If this is done, similar modelling suggests that the actual 2004/05 system produces almost identical *average* household incomes to an earnings adjusted 1997 system (Hills, 2004a, fig. 9.5). Overall, New Labour's reforms have been fiscally neutral compared with the hypothetical 'Old Labour' alternative. However, the bottom five-tenths of the income distribution as a whole are better off with New Labour's reforms than they would have been under earnings indexation, while the top four-tenths are worse off. On this kind of comparison, New Labour's reforms actually come out as more clearly redistributive from those with high incomes to those with low incomes (especially to families with children).

The contribution of social science to the recent debate

During the 1980s and indeed right up to 1997, the discussion of 'poverty' passed out of official currency. This was despite – or even because of – the way in which government policies were compounding the growth of inequality. But at the same time poverty re-emerged as a focus for social research in a way it had not done since the nineteenth century and the 1960s. Strikingly, an important facilitator was television.

London Weekend Television commissioned the polling organisation MORI to conduct a survey as background to a series of four programmes on 'Breadline Britain'. Two of the programme's writers, Joanna Mack and Stewart Lansley, discussed the survey with social policy academics – Vic George, Peter Townsend, David Piachaud, Richard Berthoud and Peter Taylor-Gooby, a roll call of the leading poverty analysts of the day. They came up not just with a new survey, but a new conceptual approach to the whole problem. As we discussed in chapter 5, Townsend (1979) had argued that poverty was socially constructed and depended on individuals' capacity to be included in the mainstream of society. The question was, how to decide which activities and items were necessary for such inclusion? What income was needed for participation? Townsend's view (1979, ch. 6) was that he could construct such a line statistically from consumption patterns. Others disagreed, arguing that, in the end, poverty was a subjective social measure of what people thought was a minimum below which people should not live. The way to find that out was to ask the population, not just rely on experts. The approach of Mack and Lansley (1985) was to ask a sample of the whole population what items they thought were necessities, and then use majority views of this to define which items people should not go without. They could then identify who was poor as lacking such necessities because they could not afford them. This approach has since been repeated in other studies, including the 1999 Poverty and Social Exclusion Survey of Britain (Gordon et al., 2000).

This approach owed much to the work of Amartya Sen (1983), an economist whose work included the study of famines and who had debated the concept of poverty with Townsend in the 1960s. There is, Sen argued, an 'absolutist core' to poverty. Starvation and death are not relative concepts, and in the developing world they are the key to poverty. Yet his work provided a framework that took the debate beyond just 'absolute' versus 'relative' concepts of need. Adam Smith had framed poverty in terms of being able to 'appear in public without shame'. Sen's 'capabilities' framework developed the way in which such benchmarks for participation depended on the society and time within which people lived. This has had a major influence on the notions of poverty employed by the United Nations Development Programme in its annual reports and on the UN Copenhagen Agreement in 1995. This committed signatories to eradicating poverty through national actions and international cooperation. It distinguished 'absolute' and 'overall' poverty and led to attempts to give these terms distinct meanings (Gordon et al., 2000; Gordon and Townsend, 2000).

Within the UK, evidence accumulated through the 1980s of the extent to which there had been a dramatic shift in income distribution, not least from official statistics such as the new Households Below Average Income analysis. In 1992 the Joseph Rowntree Foundation commissioned a programme to research this and bring all the evidence together, and also an Inquiry Group chaired by one of its trustees, Sir Peter Barclay, to consider the implications of the findings (Barclay, 1995; Hills, 1995). When the Inquiry Group's report was published in 1995, its findings and concerns resonated widely; indeed public concerns about the gap between rich and poor reached a peak that year. As in Charles Booth's and Seebohm Rowntree's time, hard empirical evidence made such concerns more difficult to ignore.

Summary

The last quarter century has seen large swings in policy towards poverty. The priority of fighting poverty was greatly reduced in the 1980s, and reforms were made to social security, taxation and public spending that were intended to improve incentives and economic growth. As unemployment grew and society changed, many more people found themselves depending on social security benefits that were falling behind average living standards. As a result of both factors, poverty grew. However social spending remained much the same share of national income, and the growth of means testing had negative effects on incentives, both despite the intentions of the reforms. Since 1997, New Labour has followed a mixture of policies, with reducing child and pensioner poverty of increasing importance. Its macroeconomic success in maintaining steady growth and falling unemployment has helped, but it has had to grapple with much the same underlying pressures and dilemmas – specifically how to make progress against poverty when there are escalating demands on social spending for other purposes, and when political pressure to keep down tax rates remains as tight as ever. It is to such pressures that we turn in the next chapter, and then in the final chapter to ways in which this conflict might work out over the next 20 years.

Part III
Looking forward

7 Policy challenges and dilemmas for the next 20 years

John Hills

Where are we now? The UK in international perspective

One of the factors which has helped push poverty, particularly child poverty, up the policy agenda in recent years has been the body of evidence on Britain's comparatively dismal record by comparison with other countries.[1] Table 11 gives the position in 15 comparable countries (members of the European Union or of the 'G7' major industrialised countries) in 2000 or the nearest available year, based on Luxembourg Income Study analysis of national data sources on a comparable basis. It shows poverty rates based on a line of 60 per cent of each country's own median income, together with a measure of severe poverty (numbers below a line of 40 per cent of median income in each country).

Overall, only the US and Ireland had worse relative poverty rates, only the US had a worse child poverty rate, and only Ireland a worse poverty rate for its elderly population. In four countries, the child poverty rate was less than half that in the UK, and in two the poverty rate for the elderly was less than half that here. Against the severe threshold of 40 per cent of median income, the UK was not so far above the average, but its level was still the fourth worst shown. By contrast, in one of the earliest uses of this data source, Mitchell (1991) found that in the late 1970s and early 1980s, the UK had the lowest poverty rate against a severe poverty line out of the 10 countries examined.

Table 11: **International comparison of relative poverty rates, 2000 or late 1990s (% of population)**

	Below 60% of population median			Below 40% of median
	All	*Children*	*Elderly*	
United States (2000)	23.8	30.2	33.3	10.8
Ireland (1996)	21.8	23.6	41.5	4.0
United Kingdom (1999)	21.3	27.0	34.9	5.7
Italy (2000)	19.9	26.5	22.2	7.3
Canada (1998)	19.7	23.8	21.5	7.6
Denmark (1997)	17.1	14.5	30.5	5.7
Belgium (1997)	14.4	13.7	22.7	3.3
Austria (1997)	14.2	17.3	22.7	3.3
France (1994)	14.1	14.3	18.5	3.4
Germany (2000)	13.1	11.2	21.2	4.9
Netherlands (1999)	12.7	14.8	12.8	4.6
Luxembourg (2000)	12.5	18.3	10.5	1.4
Finland (2000)	12.4	8.0	24.8	2.1
Norway (2000)	12.3	7.5	28.9	2.9
Sweden (2000)	12.3	9.2	21.2	3.8

Source: Hills (2004a), table 3.6 (based on Luxembourg Income Study).

From some perspectives a poor performance in relative poverty rates might be seen as less serious if a country's income was so high that the absolute standard of living of its poor population was still high by comparison with living standards elsewhere. However, analysis by UNICEF (2000) of the position in the mid 1990s suggests that even on this kind of comparison the UK was doing badly in terms of child poverty. It calculated child poverty rates against a fixed international standard, based on the US poverty line (converted at purchasing power parities). This showed the UK to have a child poverty rate of 29 per cent against this standard, better only than that in Italy and Spain within the EU, and twice the rate in the US.[2]

There are now indications that the UK's international position is improving. Figure 18, for instance, shows that in the indicators published by the European Commission, the UK moved from having the worst relative child poverty rate in the EU in the year up to 1997, to fifth worst in the year up to 2001. The rate in the UK fell, while it rose in most other EU countries. None the less, there was still a long way to go for the UK to fall to the EU average, let alone to reach the government's target of being 'among the best in Europe' by 2020.

The same data source suggests little change in the rate of adult poverty in the UK over that period, but a deterioration in five of the other EU members (Stewart, 2005b, fig. 14.2). Within this, there was a very slight fall in poverty among the retired population in the UK, but this contrasted with increases in eight other member states.

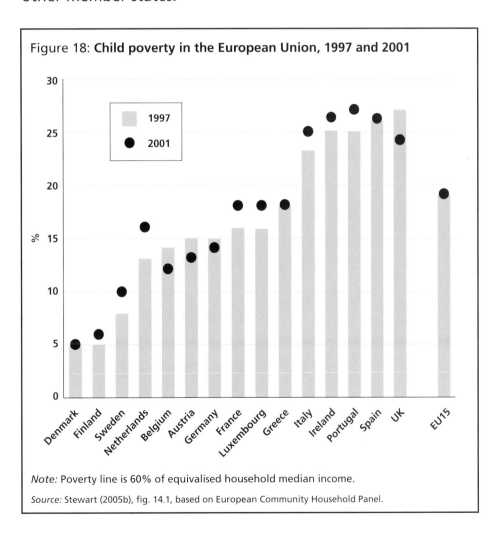

Figure 18: **Child poverty in the European Union, 1997 and 2001**

Note: Poverty line is 60% of equivalised household median income.

Source: Stewart (2005b), fig. 14.1, based on European Community Household Panel.

The picture of recent improvements in the UK, particularly against absolute standards, is confirmed by figure 19. This shows the reduction in the proportion of the population counted as poor between 1998 and 2001 within each EU member state, using both relative and absolute standards. Against a *relative* standard, the UK's performance was the best in Europe, and against an *absolute* standard it was one of the four recording the largest falls.

Ireland's position is notable here: its combination of rapid growth in average living standards combined with a smaller but still significant increase in real incomes for the poorest meant that it had both the fastest *growth* in relative poverty, and

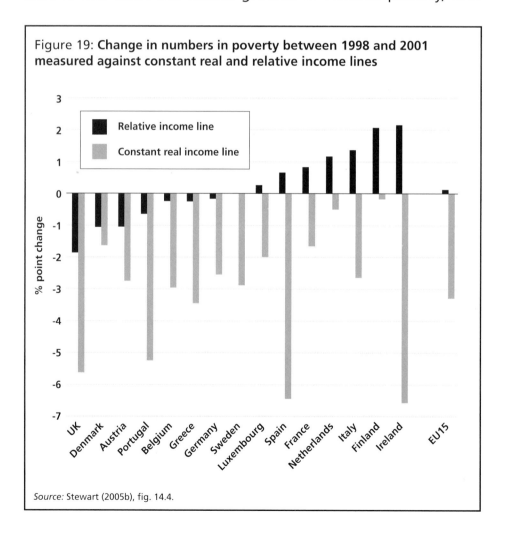

Figure 19: **Change in numbers in poverty between 1998 and 2001 measured against constant real and relative income lines**

Source: Stewart (2005b), fig. 14.4.

fastest *fall* against an absolute standard. This illustrates the importance of looking at movements in both relative and absolute incomes in trying to understand the position of the poor. Under the 'tiered' approach the British government is now taking to tracking what is happening to child poverty, it will be seen to be falling unambiguously only when *both* measures, and a third including indicators of material deprivation, are all falling (HM Treasury, 2004, p. 17).

The UK's poor record on poverty in international terms can be traced back to a number of factors, each of which gives a clue to policies that might help reduce it. First, the UK has a high proportion of households without income from work. While its recorded unemployment rate is now one of the lowest in the EU, it still has one of the largest proportions of working age adults in jobless households overall, a manifestation of the growth of economic inactivity discussed in chapter 6 (Hills, 2004a, table 3.7). Its rate of 10.9 per cent of those aged 18–59 living in jobless households in 2003 was exceeded only in Belgium. This is a particularly important driver of child poverty – in the mid 1990s a fifth of all children in the UK were in workless households, double the OCED average and the highest of 18 countries surveyed by Gregg and Wadsworth (2001). By 2003, the rate had fallen a little, but was still the highest in the EU (Hills, 2004a, table 3.7). As figure 20 shows, this is partly driven by the combination of a high rate of lone parenthood – only New Zealand and the US exceed the UK's 22 per cent rate – and the low proportion of lone parents who are employed. This latter factor has been changing recently, with a 10 percentage point increase in the employment rate of lone mothers from 44 per cent in 1996 to 54 per cent in 2002 (HM Treasury, 2003a, chart 4.4). Whether the current government's target of a 70 per cent employment rate for lone mothers by 2010 can be reached is an open question but, as the figure shows, many other countries do achieve something close to this or higher.

A second factor is the low level of social security benefits for those out of work in the UK in relation to poverty standards, in

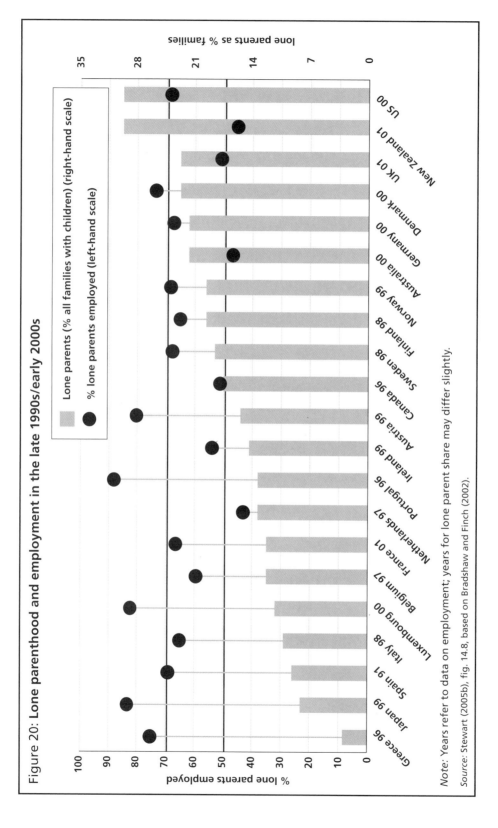

Figure 20: Lone parenthood and employment in the late 1990s/early 2000s

Note: Years refer to data on employment; years for lone parent share may differ slightly.

Source: Stewart (2005b), fig. 14.8, based on Bradshaw and Finch (2002).

European terms at least. Figure 21, based on work by Behrendt (2002), shows social assistance entitlements in relation to median incomes and hence relative poverty lines in the mid 1990s in Sweden, Britain and Germany for six different family types. In the Swedish case, social assistance rates are above the poverty line for all six cases, and in the German case in three of them, but in the UK all of them fell short (although a pensioner couple came close to it). Since then, UK social assistance (Income Support) rates have fallen further behind median incomes for most of these cases, although they have improved recently for families with children and pensioners. For a lone parent with two children, Income Support rates exceeded 60 per cent of median income by 2004/05 (Stewart, 2005b, fig. 14.12). But for working age adults without children, Income Support rates are well below the effective poverty line. As a result, the UK has one of the highest poverty rates for the unemployed in the EU – just under half in 2001 on the basis used by the EU,[3] compared to under 40 per cent in the EU as a whole.

But the UK also has a relatively high rate of poverty among those with income from work – 28 per cent of working single parents and 19 per cent of single earner couples in 2001, compared with EU averages of 22 and 20 per cent respectively (Stewart, 2005b, fig. 14.9). In the case of lone parents, this reflects the gender gap in pay generally, but also high rates of part-time working and the particularly low rates of pay for women working part-time in the UK (Harkness and Waldfogel, 2003).

But the UK's problem of low pay is wider than this. As figure 22 shows, the UK had one of the largest increases in wage inequality between 1980 and 2000 of the ten countries shown – only New Zealand and the US had a larger increase, and three of the ten had a decline. This divergence in experiences suggests that we cannot look solely for global explanations for the increase in the incidence of low pay in the UK. It is true that unskilled workers in many industrialised countries have been hit by 'skill biased technological change', and this has driven

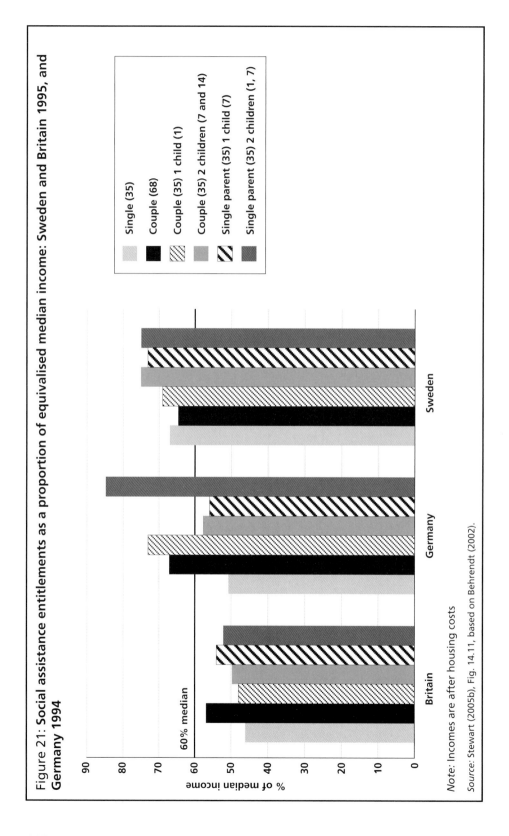

Figure 21: Social assistance entitlements as a proportion of equivalised median income: Sweden and Britain 1995, and Germany 1994

Note: Incomes are after housing costs

Source: Stewart (2005b), Fig. 14.11, based on Behrendt (2002).

both unemployment and relative wages (Hills, 2004a, ch. 4). But the UK has been hit worse than most. First, institutional restraints on low pay weakened in the 1980s – both through the decline of trade unions and the abolition of limited wage protection through the wages councils. Second, Britain had a relatively large number of unqualified workers to start with, and therefore a larger proportion of the population was potentially affected by both technological change and developments in world trade. The UK's unequal earnings distribution is related to its unequal distribution of skills.[4] These

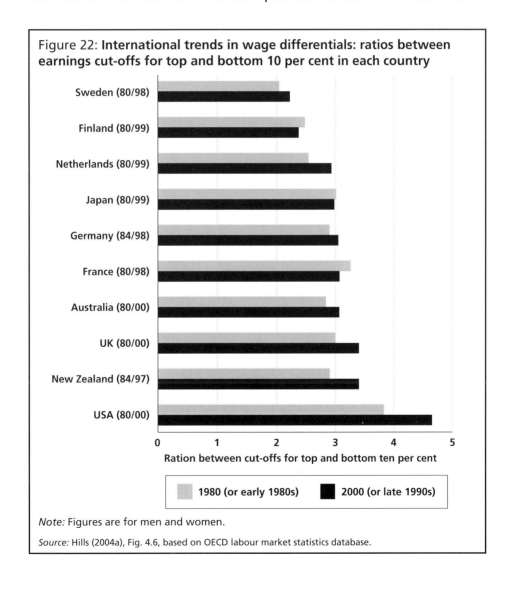

Figure 22: **International trends in wage differentials: ratios between earnings cut-offs for top and bottom 10 per cent in each country**

Note: Figures are for men and women.

Source: Hills (2004a), Fig. 4.6, based on OECD labour market statistics database.

143

factors may interact – in countries where labour market institutions have resisted growing wage dispersion, as in continental Europe, this may have encouraged investment in technologies that have increased the productivity of less skilled workers, and hence slowed the extent to which technological change has been skill biased by comparison with, say, the US (Acemoglu, 2003).

More recently, two factors have changed in the other direction. The National Minimum Wage, introduced in 1999, may not have affected a large proportion of workers so far, but it has put a floor to further drift downwards right at the bottom. At the same time, New Labour's tax credit reforms described in the previous chapter have increased net incomes for those in low paid work, particularly, but not only, those with children. By 2001 the UK had one of the most generous 'child benefit packages' in the world for low paid workers, if we look across support through the tax and benefit system and help with housing costs for families with children, compared with those without children (Stewart, 2005b, table 14.2, based on analysis in Bradshaw and Finch, 2002). This is a considerable improvement on earlier international comparisons in the 1980s and 1990s (although the means tested nature of the UK system means that it is around the international average in terms of support for families with children and on average earnings).

Finally, one feature of poverty in the UK – and in the US – that stands out from recent international comparisons is that when it occurs, poverty is more likely to be persistent here than in some other comparable countries. For instance, an OECD comparison of poverty durations in the early 1990s suggested that for those who were affected by poverty in a six year period, the average duration was 2.4 years or less in the Netherlands, Sweden, Germany and Canada, but 3.0 years or more in the UK and US (Oxley, Dang and Antolín, 1999). Accelerating the rate at which those who fall into poverty can escape it would have a major effect on the proportion of the UK population who are poor at any one time.

What do we want? Public attitudes, poverty and policy

In considering how policy towards poverty might develop, a crucial factor is what the public as a whole thinks – either because policy makers will have to operate within the constraints of those attitudes, or because attitudes might have to change before policy can follow. Here responses to the long-running British Social Attitudes (BSA) survey have given very enlightening information, now stretching over 20 years.[5]

First, the survey has consistently shown unhappiness with the extent of income inequality in Britain. For instance, in 2002, 82 per cent of respondents to the survey said they thought that 'the gap between those with high incomes and those with low incomes is too large', with only 13 per cent thinking it is 'about right', and very few that it is too small. The proportion agreeing is higher now than it was 20 years ago, when income inequality itself was less, but even in 1983 more than 70 per cent agreed (Hills, 2004a, fig. 2.11). Furthermore, this inequality is not seen as functional: in 1999, 54 per cent of respondents rejected the idea that 'large differences in income are necessary for Britain's prosperity', with only 17 per cent agreeing (Jowell et al., 2000, p. 324).

Second, the survey produces support for the idea that people see 'poverty' as being at least in some way related to contemporary living standards. When offered three definitions of poverty, around 60 per cent of the population say that someone would be in poverty if they had 'enough to eat and live, but not enough to buy other things they needed' (Hills, 2004a, table 3.8). This is clearly more than a bare subsistence level, but how much more – and how what constitutes 'poverty' changes over time – will depend on what people class as 'needs'. Here the results of the 1999 Poverty and Social Exclusion Survey of Britain (PSE survey) indicate that as general prosperity grows, so does the range of goods and activities that people see as necessities. The PSE survey asked, as did the earlier 'Breadline Britain' surveys in 1983 and 1990, whether people thought that particular activities or possessions were 'necessary, which all adults should be able to afford and which they should not have to go without'. For instance, in 1983 only 43 per cent thought that a telephone was a necessity; by 1999 72 per cent thought it was (Gordon et al., 2000, table 12). Similarly, in the 1983 and 1990 surveys, fewer than 40 per cent thought that the ability to 'have friends and family round for a meal, snack or drink' was a necessity; by 1999 65 per cent thought that it was.

Further evidence that people see poverty in largely relative terms can be seen in table 12. When asked what they thought had happened to poverty over the previous ten years, half of respondents in 1986 and 1989 said it had been increasing – two thirds in 1994 – and just under a third that it was steady – a quarter in 1994. Few thought it had been decreasing. By 2000, roughly equal numbers thought poverty had been steady over the 1990s as thought it had increased. Looking back at table 10 and figure 16 in the last chapter, these perceptions are consistent with the trends shown in poverty against a relative line. They are not consistent with people taking an absolute view – if they had, they would have reported poverty as decreasing in the ten-year periods up to 1994 and particularly up to 2000.

As to the level of the poverty line, the BSA survey regularly asks respondents whether people receiving particular benefits or with certain incomes have enough to live on. Two features of the results are notable. First, when asked about people receiving benefits while unemployed, respondents are more likely to say they have enough to live on than when they are told the actual weekly income the benefits give (although in both cases a majority say the people would not have enough to live on). Second, the results suggest that when asked about the incomes equating to the 60 per cent of median income line, about half of respondents say this is enough to live on, about half that it is not (Hills, 2004a, table 3.13). Below these levels, large proportions say that income is not enough to live on. In other words, the closest we have to an 'official' poverty line

Table 12: **Perceptions of trends in poverty in Britain over past ten years, 1986–2000, GB (%)**

	1986	*1989*	*1994*	*2000*
Increasing	51	50	68	37
Staying at same level	30	31	24	38
Decreasing	15	16	6	20
Base	*1548*	*1516*	*1167*	*3426*

Source: Hills (2004a), table 3.11, based on British Social Attitudes survey.

appears roughly in line with the views of the median respondent.[6]

Agreement that poverty exists and has been increasing does not necessarily mean that people think government should do something about it. However, in 2000 only 23 per cent blamed 'laziness or lack of willpower' for people's own poverty. The majority blamed factors outside individual control – bad luck (15 per cent); 'an inevitable part of modern life' (34 per cent); and 'injustice in our society' (21 per cent) (Hills, 2004a, table 3.14). It is true that the proportion blaming individual factors is higher than in earlier years (19 per cent in 1986 and 1994, and 15 per cent in 1994), and the proportion doing so is the highest in the European Union apart from Portugal (Gallie and Paugam, 2002). However, most people in the UK clearly see poverty as the result of factors outside individual control.[7] Furthermore, only 28 per cent respondents to the BSA in 1994 agreed that, 'British governments nowadays can do very little to reduce poverty'; 70 per cent thought they could do 'quite a bit'. Since the 1980s, a majority has agreed – 58 per cent in 2000 – that 'it is the responsibility of government to reduce the difference in income between people with high incomes and people with low incomes'. In 1998, just over half (53 per cent) said that 'government should increase taxes on the better-off to spend more on the poor', with only a sixth preferring an alternative statement that 'the better-off pay too much tax already' (Hills and Lelkes, 1999).

All this suggests public backing for anti-poverty policies – if they too can go with the grain of public opinion. In selecting policies governments may be more constrained, as table 13 suggests. When people are asked whether government should spend more on 'welfare benefits' for the poor, even if it means higher taxes, more agree (44 per cent in 2002) than disagree (26 per cent). But the balance in favour has narrowed since the 1980s and early 1990s. Similarly, the balance, while still in favour, of the proposition that 'government should redistribute income from the better-off to those who are less well-off' has also narrowed over the period. The most important items within the social security budget – pensions, benefits for disabled people, and support for families with children on low wages – command support for increases, but benefits for the unemployed do not. Scepticism about the latter appears to reflect worries about the disincentive effects of benefits and the extent of fraud that became stronger over the 1990s (Hills, 2004a, figs 6.11–13). Instead, people believe that government should make sure that anyone who can work should be guaranteed a job. In short, the New Labour slogan of 'work for those who can, security for those who cannot' has strong public

Table 13: **Attitudes towards redistribution and welfare benefits, 1987–2002, GB (%)**

	1987	1989	1991	1993	1994	1996	1998	2000	2002
Government should spend more money on welfare benefits for the poor									
Agree	55	61	58	53	50	43	43	38	44
Neither	23	23	23	25	25	29	29	31	27
Disagree	22	15	18	20	23	26	26	30	26
Government should redistribute income to the less well-off									
Agree	45	50	49	45	51	44	39	39	39
Neither	20	20	20	21	23	26	28	24	25
Disagree	33	29	29	33	25	28	31	36	34
Base	1281	2604	2481	2567	2929	3085	2531	2980	2929

Source: Hills (2004a), table 8.3, based on British Social Attitudes survey.

resonance. Whether what is being done to deliver it is enough, and whether views would be different if there was wider knowledge of just how low some benefit levels are, are different questions.

The unfinished agenda? The JRF Income and Wealth Inquiry ten years on

In February 1995 the Joseph Rowntree Foundation's Income and Wealth Inquiry Group, chaired by Sir Peter Barclay, published its report. The group, with a broadly based membership, had been convened by the Foundation as evidence accumulated on the extent to which income inequality and relative poverty had grown since the late 1970s.[8] It reviewed evidence, both from official sources and from a research programme specially commissioned by the Foundation. Most of the statistical evidence available then covered the period up to between 1991 and 1993.

The group concluded that 'Policy-makers should be concerned with the way in which the living standards of a substantial minority of the population have lagged behind since the late 1970s. Not only is this a problem for those directly affected, it also damages the social fabric and so affects us all' (Barclay, 1995, p. 8). Given that conclusion, the group produced a wide-ranging series of recommendations, headline versions of which are listed in box 3. As well as this list of specific measures, the Inquiry Group argued that 'It is hard to overstate the importance of raising education and training standards in Britain . . . Nor is it a matter of choosing where to redirect existing resources at the expense of currently favoured sectors; greater investment is required at virtually every level' (Barclay, 1995, p. 10). Tony Blair's three priorities of 'education, education, and education' before the 1997 election sounded a similar note (although the new investment did not come until after 1999).

149

Box 3 **Recommendations of the 1995 JRF Income and Wealth Inquiry Group**

Recommendation	*Outcome*
Labour market	
1 Direct provision of employment opportunities.	No.
2 Greatly increased childcare provision.	Yes – but more emphasis on subsidies than provision.
3 More flexibility in working time.	Can now request.
4 Strengthened legislation against discrimination, including disabled people.	Yes (e.g. Disability Discrimination Act).
5 Subsidies to take on long term unemployed.	In New Deal.
6 Minimum wage and/or more in-work benefits.	Both.
7 Review of social security for part-timers and self employed.	No.
Social security – out of work	
8 Benefits should rise by more than inflation.	Generally inflation only, unless have children.
9 More Social Fund grants, not loans.	Increases in funds for some forms of grant.

Recommendation	Outcome
10 If on benefit:	
(a) Relaxed rules on education;	No major change.
(b) More work training with allowances;	Training options under New Deals.
(c) No 'long term' unemployment without work offer;	In New Deal.
(d) Training guarantee;	In New Deal.
(e) Wider entitlement for 16–17 year olds;	No.
(f) Easier to do voluntary work.	Partly.
11 Think again about 6 month limit on non-means tested Jobseeker's Allowance.	No.
12 Disregard of maintenance in Income Support.	*New* Income Support recipients have £10 of maintenance receipts disregarded, and maintenance is disregarded for tax credits.
Between benefits and work	
13 Speed up calculation and payment of in-work benefits.	New structure of Child Tax Credit means payment continues on move into low-paid work, but initial problems with tax credit administration. Some benefit 'run-ons' extended.

Recommendation	Outcome
14 Easier reactivation of Income Support claims.	Yes.
15 More publicity for 'trial periods' in work.	Yes.
16 Fixed allowance for long term benefit recipients trying to get back to work.	Principle of fund available for both benefits and other costs of getting to work is part of Employment Zones.
17 Lump sum payment on return to work.	Yes – £100 Job Grant (and complex system of back-to-work bonus for those with earnings while on benefit).
18 Higher earnings disregard in Income Support, with possibility to accumulate over 6 weeks.	No.
19 Disregard of childcare and work expenses.	Childcare tax credit now helps with childcare costs in work.
20 Restore free school meals to those on Family Credit.	No.
21 Reduced benefit withdrawal rates in Family Credit and Housing Benefit.	Reduced for Child Tax Credit and Working Tax Credit, but not for Housing Benefit (although reduced for those 'floated off' Housing Benefit).

Recommendation	Outcome
Pensions	
22 Need for political consensus.	No.
23 'Clear encouragement' for all income groups to accumulate private pension rights.	Incentive for additional accumulation increased for some as a result of Pension Credit, but reduced for others.
24 Avoid extension of means testing.	No – means testing widened.
25 Floor to retirement incomes rising faster than price indexation.	Yes – on means tested basis, if Guarantee Credit claimed.
Taxation	
26 Reduced share of tax on low incomes.	Yes – if tax credits included.
27 Restructuring of National Insurance contributions for low paid.	Yes.
28 Review of taxation of charities and greater incentives to donate.	'Gift Aid' easier.
Housing	
29 Social rent levels should be moderated.	Depends on comparator.
30 (a) Avoid concentrated allocations;	'Choice-based lettings' in some areas.
(b) New developments – tenure mix.	In part.

Recommendation	Outcome
Marginalised areas	
31 Need for strategy to revitalise marginalised areas.	Yes – National Strategy for Neighbourhood Renewal.
32 Specific items:	
(a) Involvement of business leaders;	Represented on Local Strategic Partnerships, but without a major role.
(b) Training link with employers;	Some examples.
(c) Local managers with decentralised budgets and resident involvement;	Within some initiatives, not others.
(d) Long-term support workers;	Not many examples.
(e) Resident training;	Yes – 'capacity building' programmes.
(f) Radical improvement in local schools;	Improvement in primary schools; less evidence in secondary schools.
(g) Positive role for young people;	Some examples, such as 'Young Movers'.
(h) Improved transport;	Very variable.
(i) Economic regeneration for certain regions beyond estate initiatives.	Limited.

Alongside the list in the box is a short note of what has happened to related policy since then. This gives a convenient checklist against which to compare recent policy developments summarised in the previous chapter. An immediate observation is that there is a substantial overlap between the Inquiry Group's recommendations and policy as it has developed since 1997. Roughly half of the 46 recommendations itemised in the box have been adopted largely as suggested, and only 8 have clearly not been followed. In some respects policy has gone further than the Inquiry Group argued for – notably perhaps the child poverty commitments and structure of the new tax credits, the labour market measures associated with the New Deal, and some aspects of the National Strategy for Neighbourhood Renewal. The differences also highlight some key features of New Labour policy:

- Policy as it has developed has more emphasis on means testing than implied by the Inquiry Group, particularly for pensioners, but also for the unemployed.
- While low income pensioners and those with children have benefited from above inflation increases in benefits (and tax credits), working age people without children have not.
- While the New Deals have gone further in many ways than the Inquiry Group programme, there has not been much by way of 'direct provision of employment opportunities', and the benefit treatment of those remaining unemployed has generally remained tougher than several of the Group's recommendations suggested.
- Policy has covered a wider range of issues than touched on by the Inquiry Group, for instance, in some of the groups of vulnerable young people focused on by the Social Exclusion Unit and related policy change, the emphasis now being given to early years policy, and the attention – if limited specific action[9] – devoted to health inequalities.

A striking feature of New Labour has been the *lack* of emphasis on inequality overall – between top and bottom – as a focus of policy since 1997, as opposed to the strong focus on inequality between the bottom and the middle. What is also clear is that despite the many areas in which there have been policy initiatives, there are still gaps. The discussion above highlights the position of working age adults without children who are dependent on benefits. Other groups have also had their rights *reduced* by other aspects of government policy – most notably asylum seekers (Burchardt, 2005): the commitment to 'inclusion' has, literally, had borders.

Constraints and pressures on future policy

Public opinion is not the only constraint on policy makers. Looking ahead, there is little sign that life will become easier for those trying to reconcile public demands for a more equal society, public services that meet the demands of an ageing and more affluent society, and political constraints on resources available through taxation.[10]

The most obvious pressure comes from an ageing society. It is not inherent in increased life expectancy that social spending should increase as a share of income. After all, one could imagine a world in which the ages at which all events related to economic activity and social needs grew in proportion – ages of entering education, leaving education and entering the labour force, retirement, onset of greater medical and care needs, and eventual mortality. The overall balance between social spending and national income could stay the same without strain – but with periods at work and periods receiving transfers in cash and kind lengthened in proportion. But as things have developed and seem likely to develop, this does not appear to be happening:

• There is no sign of delay in entering education, quite the reverse, but ages to which people remain in education are rising.

- Retirement ages have begun to creep back up in the last ten years, but had previously *fallen* rather than risen as life expectancies increased. Expectations for the future are still dominated by the idea of retirement at a particular age – say, 65 – rather than one which relates to growing life expectancies.
- Britain's population structure has not been in a steady state. Fertility rates have been in decline long term. This has been masked by the 'baby boom' generation, born after the Second World War, but when this generation reaches 65, the ratio between those aged over 65 and those of working age will rise sharply.
- We simply do not know how health and long term care needs will develop as the population ages. An optimistic view would be that needs would be delayed until people were older – this would actually put off needs for social spending, and help the public finances. Alternatively, such needs could remain the same for people of any given age, and so pressures on social spending would increase fast as a greater proportion of the population exceeded any given age.

At the same time, the presumption that we will continue to become a more affluent society does not necessarily help things. If we could keep the salaries of doctors, teachers, nurses and road-menders fixed indefinitely in real terms, the cost of providing public services might fall in relation to national income. However, the evidence is that if public sector pay lags behind other incomes, there is eventually a period of catch-up to cope with the problems of quality, retention, recruitment and low morale. Equally, if productivity in providing services grew fast enough, the share of GDP required could fall. The problem is not necessarily that productivity does not improve – but rather that public expectations for service quality, based on experience elsewhere in the economy, rise just as fast. Even worse, the very services where public provision is important – health care and education – are ones to which people appear to want to devote an *increasing* proportion of their resources as they become better off. As a result, quite apart from any factors associated with ageing or tackling disadvantage, one might expect the demands for social spending to rise as a share of national income over time. There certainly seems little reason to assume that they will fall as a result of economic growth.

Similarly, if we saw poverty in absolute terms, tackling it would become easier as real incomes grew. Funding social security benefits merely with a stable *real* value while incomes (and taxes) are growing reduces the pressure on public finances quite considerably, as we know from the last 20 years. However, the evidence reviewed above suggests that views of poverty and inclusion actually relate to contemporary living standards. The real cost of relieving poverty in these terms rises as incomes rise – unless other factors move rapidly in the right direction, and incomes from other sources fill the gap.

To give an idea of the magnitude of these pressures, we can calculate what would happen to social spending if we carried on in future spending the same amount on each person of a given age as we do now in relation to average incomes, allowing for current official projections of the future age structure of the population. Looking just at health, education and social security, this would imply spending rising from 21.8 per cent of GDP in 2001 to 26.3 per cent of GDP in 2051 (Hills, 2004a, table 10.2). For some this will be seen as clearly feasible – it is an increase of less than 0.4 per cent per year, and much of the increase in health spending is already built into government plans, for instance. For others, if translated into today's money, it would mean extra spending – and taxes – eventually of an amount equivalent to £50 billion per year, a politically very alarming figure if it was needed all at once. There are reasons why fiscal life might be easier – the projected increase in life expectancy might turn out to be mostly of 'healthy' life, for instance, and both retirement ages and the age of onset of health care needs could both rise. But there are probably more factors that would make things harder – the calculation does not allow for making progress in reducing poverty, or for rising long term care needs. The latter could be substantial.[11]

One of the things we do not know is whether the other factors referred to above will 'move in the right direction', that is in ways that reduce the market inequalities that the social security and tax credit systems end up compensating for. Economic growth in the last 20 years in the UK and US has been associated with widening market inequalities. However, this has not been the case in other countries, and in previous eras the presumption was that income inequality would *reduce* as economies developed. It would be optimistic to assume that the trends of the last few years will suddenly reverse. On the other hand, these trends are not inevitable, and policies towards the labour market, minimum wages, skills, education, discrimination, childhood poverty, disadvantaged areas and investment may all make a difference to people's ability to derive incomes from the market.

Some of the pressures on the public finances can be kept in check while making progress on poverty if there is more reliance on 'targeting' services and benefits on the poorest. Indeed, this has been an important part of the story of the last seven years. But there are limits to how far this can be pushed. On the one hand, figure 13 has already shown the wide income range across which the quite high effective marginal tax rates associated with the new tax credits now stretch. On top of these come other income tested transfers from the state – Education Maintenance Allowances for families with 16–17 year olds; student finance support worth at least £3,000 a year for students from families with low or moderate incomes by comparison with those with higher incomes; or repayment of student loans at a rate of 9 per cent of earnings above a threshold. Some families will face more than one of these at once. Adding to them through further income testing means either deepening or widening what was once the 'poverty trap' but which now affects those with incomes nearer to the average.

There is also a political problem: if the government is raising taxes to improve public services, but all of the proceeds are concentrated on the poorest, many voters will see little return for their money. Of course, ensuring that the poorest gain disproportionately is the aim of a poverty reduction strategy. But a policy of 'progressive universalism' as New Labour has tagged it (and has delivered in the case of support for children), means that spending has to increase even faster than under a policy where general needs are kept up with, but nothing extra is done for the poor.

All of this leaves policy makers with some acute dilemmas: there is public backing for a continuing assault on poverty, but both the instruments and resources available to mount it look likely to be even more tightly constrained in the next few years. In the final chapter we discuss alternative ways in which these pressures may play out.

Part IV
Conclusions

8 Poverty and progress for the next generation?

More complex and difficult

When Seebohm Rowntree was writing a century ago he could talk about poverty as it affected a relatively homogeneous working class population in the town, York, that he studied. What drove poverty could be narrowed down to a fairly narrow set of factors, several of them related to variations in needs and earnings capacity over the life cycle – large families, loss of earnings due to sickness and old age without any other income source.

Sixty years ago, Beveridge could take results from Rowntree's 1899 and 1936 surveys to suggest that poverty could be tackled without much by way of redistribution between social classes through the combination of a social insurance system covering old age and risks of unemployment and sickness, together with a system of family allowances and a National Health Service. Problems related to the life cycle and to risks to which most were exposed could be dealt with through life cycle redistribution and insurance. Even then, Beveridge was skating over the problems of low pay and of what could really be achieved without progressive ways of raising money and redistribution between classes.

Today both the drivers of poverty and the policies that might be marshalled to tackle it are more diverse, and the politics of doing so correspondingly more complicated. Wider conceptualisations of disadvantage increase the dimensions across which failure to achieve inclusion is seen as a problem. Problems have changed their shape as well – in 1899 children in large families represented a major cost in money and cause of poverty; now families are smaller but children also represent a *time* cost that leads to earnings forgone for some parents but also pressured lives for others.

But we have done better

So one conclusion from this review of the last century is that some of the issues have become more complex. A second is that increasing affluence by itself does not solve the problems or necessarily make it easier for policy makers to do so. A third is, however, that there have been periods when we have done much better than recently. The post-war welfare state and full employment may not have led to quite the abolition of poverty suggested by Rowntree's flawed analysis of his third survey of York in 1950, but they certainly led to major progress by comparison with the first half of the twentieth century. The records of the Labour governments of the 1960s and 1970s were criticised at the time for slow progress in reducing poverty and inequality, but some aspects of their records look enviable today.[1]

A common factor in the periods of progress – and in the areas where undoubted progress has been made since the mid 1990s – is that policies have simultaneously tackled the 'causes of social ills' *and* worked to address their ill effects. Where it has been assumed that poverty can be tackled through just one of these, or that they are alternatives, we have been much less successful. Hoping that economic growth will trickle down to the poor or that welfare-to-work programmes by themselves will solve working age poverty without any change in the incomes of those remaining out of work have not worked. But nor have strategies relying only on the redistribution of income to ameliorate the impact of market income inequalities that reflect much deeper differences in economic opportunity. This is not just because the underlying problems are left untouched, but also because political support for such a strategy is much harder to marshal.

The dynamics of anti-poverty policy

Rowntree's insights in identifying the relationship between the risk of poverty and the life cycle can be seen as an early example of social science concern with the dynamics of poverty. Recent analysis of this kind helps suggest fruitful areas for policy, whether it is addressing intergenerational links between childhood circumstances and later disadvantage, or the factors associated with short term movements in and out of poverty. This kind of approach also suggests that we should not be seeing 'passive' and 'active' social policies as alternatives. Rather we should be thinking about whether we have policies that tackle all four of the quadrants shown in figure 23, which divides policies according to whether they are concerned with affecting the risk of something happening or affecting its impact when it does, and whether they are concerned with adverse or positive events. This suggests that policies can have one or more of the following impacts:

- *Prevention* of an event or reduction of the risk of entering an undesirable state – for instance, training to improve job retention, or adaptations at work or in working patterns so that people can continue working after the onset of an impairment or a change in demands on them for caring.
- *Promotion* of exit or escape – for instance, 'welfare to work' policies to help people move out of unemployment or economic inactivity.
- *Protection* from the impact of an event, for instance paying benefits to those who become unemployed.
- *Propulsion* away from adverse circumstances by reinforcing the benefits of exit – for instance, the effects of the in-work benefits on the incomes of those leaving unemployment, or post-employment support to ensure that the next career move is upwards.

Figure 23: **Four forms of intervention**

		Intervention to change	
		Risk of event	**Effects of event**
Focus of intervention	**Entry to adverse state**	Prevention	Protection
	Exit from adverse state	Promotion	Propulsion

Importantly, policies can have more than one of these impacts at the same time. For instance, paying benefits and tax credits to low income families with children may be 'protective' today but may also have long run 'preventive' effects if children are no longer growing up in poverty.

Gaps and challenges

From this point of view one of the great strengths of policy towards poverty and social exclusion since 1997 has been that it has been multifaceted, and the most promising parts of it – for instance those concerned with childhood disadvantage – have indeed begun to address all four of these impacts of intervention at once. Given the multiplicity of drivers of poverty, it makes sense to address it with multiple policies. It is hard to see anything in the current policy mix of which we need *less* if we are to make real progress (Hills and Stewart, 2005). But there are gaps and challenges still to address, some of which we have touched on in earlier chapters:

- Continuing high levels of economic inactivity and numbers of working age households that are jobless. The initial impact of the 'New Deals' appears to have slowed (McKnight, 2005).
- Benefit incomes of those without children who are out of work. The group in poverty that are deepest in poverty – have the largest 'poverty gap' – are single adults without children,[2] unsurprising given the level of their benefits in relation to the poverty line shown in figure 21. Income Support for a single

adult is now lower than the support given for a family's first child – and the gap will widen since the former is price linked, but the latter earnings linked.

- The very low wages of many women working part-time.
- Achievement levels in secondary schools in poor areas.
- Particularly high rates of poverty among particular groups – for instance, those from certain ethnic minorities, and disabled people – reflecting a mixture of problems encompassing both discrimination and levels of skills and qualifications.
- Pensioners who fail to take up the income that should be guaranteed by the 'guarantee credit' in Pension Credit, particularly older women.

An optimistic view

Looking ahead it is possible to take optimistic or pessimistic views of how policy towards poverty will develop over the next 20 years. On an optimistic view, policies will begin to establish a virtuous circle, as measures aimed at tackling the causes of poverty start to change underlying inequalities, reducing the numbers dependent on state assistance, and so freeing up resources to allow more generous treatment of those who remain so and the extension of policies to cover current gaps. Thus if policies succeeded in raising the skills of disadvantaged young people and in reducing the economic disconnection of the most disadvantaged areas, incomes from work of the otherwise poor would rise, and the costs of social security benefits and tax credits for them would fall. This could liberate resources[3] to improve the value of benefits to those receiving them, also reinforcing the political will to do so, backed by the public desire for governments to reduce poverty discussed in chapter 7. While the demographic pressures on social spending will be upwards, reductions in economic inactivity, increases in the average age of retirement,[4] and 'healthy ageing' would make them easier to cope with. This could make possible a more general strategy of 'progressive universalism' under which social provision improves for all, but most for the poor, making gradually rising taxation acceptable – all taxpayers would be getting something for their money, while seeing poverty falling.

A pessimistic view

On a bleaker, pessimistic view, any success in tackling underlying inequalities would come too slowly to counter continuing polarisation of economic opportunities. Those without access to capital, home ownership and good education for their children would fall further behind – widening wealth inequalities would continue to reinforce intergenerational links, for instance as those with most wealth purchase houses near good schools. Even if policy succeeded in raising the skills of some young people, the lowest wages would still be set by an increasingly cut-throat global market. While the rising cost of policies to ameliorate the effects of growing market inequality on relative incomes (such as the new tax credits) would be visible, progress in reducing poverty would be slow or non-existent, and political support for pushing such strategies further would be weakened. Rapid increases in age related demands on social spending could mean that taxes would have to rise, but without taxpayers seeing what they were getting for their money, squeezing the political headroom for more resources to tackle poverty, and pushing governments further back into means tested programmes with incomplete take-up, disincentive effects and weak political support. Reinforcing the latter, if the poor are seen as 'other' it is easy to stir up prejudice, as we saw in Britain in the nineteenth century, and as has been suggested as a reason for differences in attitudes to poverty policy in the US and Europe.[5]

Rowntree's own conclusion

There is no easy way of saying which of these scenarios is the more likely. But we are more likely to establish a virtuous circle if the need for progress on reducing poverty has a high public and political profile. Charles Booth and Seebohm Rowntree showed that sound evidence was one answer to prejudice about the poor. 'Lifting the curtain' and shining an honest light on reality in the poorest parts of our society is a contribution social scientists can continue to make.

Britain was the first country to develop poverty measures, and the science has a distinguished and influential history in this country. The early poverty researchers were businessmen who were concerned enough about social problems to devote their spare time to investigating them. Their successors have been academic sociologists, statisticians, economists and civil servants, all attempting to produce rigorous research into this thorny and complex problem. Good policy making requires solid facts to go on, but definitions of poverty are invariably subjective and can alter our impressions of the magnitude or source of the problem. Different methods lead to different results, but a general picture of the historical trends and current situation emerges. It is pessimistic in that Britain had very high poverty rates for the last 15 years of the twentieth century and still has higher poverty rates than most other European countries. It is almost inevitable that parts of society become disaffected as a result. But it is optimistic in that poverty was much reduced by the Beveridge reforms, full employment and by the sharing of national prosperity with those living on benefits in the 1960s and 1970s. Recent reforms and the decline in unemployment have also led to a reduction in poverty, particularly in child poverty. This all suggests that, if the political will is there, there is no reason why policies cannot be as effective today in further reducing poverty as they were in the past. Rowntree's own conclusion from a century ago remains apposite:

That in this land of abounding wealth, during a time of perhaps unexampled prosperity, probably more than one fourth of the population are living in poverty, is a fact which may well cause great searchings of heart. There is

surely need for a greater concentration of thought by the nation upon the wellbeing of its own people, for no civilization can be sound or stable which has at its base this mass of stunted human life. The suffering may be all but voiceless, and we may long remain ignorant of its extent and severity, but when once we realize it we see that social questions of profound importance await solution.
(1901, p. 304)

Notes

1 Introduction

1 Available in a centennial edition published in 2000.

2 This chapter draws extensively on Jo Webb's 'Always with us? The evolution of poverty in Britain, 1886–2002' (2002).

3 The discussion of the period since 1997 draws heavily on a book written alongside this one, *A more equal society? New Labour, poverty, inequality and exclusion*, edited by John Hills and Kitty Stewart (2005). More detail on some of the trends and issues discussed here can also be found in *Inequality and the state* by John Hills (2004a). Research for these books was financially supported by the Joseph Rowntree Foundation, and by the Economic and Social Research Council through its general support for the Centre for Analysis of Social Exclusion (CASE) at the London School of Economics. The authors are very grateful to our funders, to colleagues within CASE for their support and assistance, particularly to Lucinda Himeur in preparing the typescript, and to Fran Bennett and Anne Power for their advice on recent changes in the social security system and in housing policy. The views expressed, and any errors and omissions, are those of the authors alone.

2 The context for Rowntree's contribution

1 Assistance to the poor from local parishes under the Poor Law.

3 Changes in poverty

1 These are analysed in Webb (2002).

2 For the benefit of younger readers, 12 pence (d) made one shilling (s) and 20 shillings made one pound (£).

3 Hills (2001), p. 4 (see also chapter 7 below); Kilpatrick (1973); Hagenaars and Van Praag (1985).

4 Townsend's alternative deprivation indicators approach has many similarities to the budget standard method but constructs the poverty line in a less transparent manner.

4 Why has poverty changed?

1 Family Resources Survey data are Crown Copyright. For their use acknowledgement is made to the Department of Social Security, the Department for Work and Pensions, the Office for National Statistics and the UK Data Archive.

2 Households were assigned to the first of the following categories that they corresponded to: (1) widows; (2) head above pension age or permanently sick or disabled; (3) head unemployed; (4) four or more children; (5) in paid work; (6) all others. Categories are close, but not exactly the same, for the two years.

3 1901 Census, table 28; 2001 Census, table KS04; the base for both years is all aged 16 and over.

4 1901 Census, table 36; 2001 Census, table KS04.

5 *Family Spending 2001/02*, Office for National Statistics, 2003.

6 Since earnings of the servant-keeping class are not recorded, a low estimate of their earnings has been used to determine this figure; if a higher estimate were made this would reduce the figure.

7 Family Resources Survey, 2001/02.

8 Lakin (2003).

5 Poverty policy from 1900 to the 1970s

1 See a collection of retrospective views in Hills, Ditch and Glennerster (1994).

6 The last quarter century

1 See Hills and Stewart (2005) for a comprehensive discussion of policy since 1997 and its results.

2 For an assessment of the impact of these policies, see Lupton and Power (2005).

3 Note that the indices for prices and earnings used by DWP in these two series are applied at different points within the year, so the two diagrams show slightly different patterns over time.

4 Partly financed by the final abolition of the Married Couple's Allowance within income tax.

5 However, those whose incomes increase by only a relatively small amount (£2,500 in 2003/04) do not in fact have their tax credits cut back for the tax year when the increase occurs, so, for a time, effective marginal tax rates are lower than the 70 per cent figure. Equally, under the 1997/98 system, Family Credit was only adjusted every six months, so for some income ranges the impact of changing incomes was also delayed.

6 For details of how the systems result in these outcomes, see Hills (2004b).

7 In fact, many higher earners would have 'contracted out' of SERPS and would receive part of the amount shown through their occupational pension scheme in return for having paid

reduced National Insurance contributions while they were working.

8 Again, many 'contracted out' higher earners would actually receive less than this from the state, but would have had the offsetting advantage of lower National Insurance contributions when at work.

7 Policy challenges and dilemmas for the next 20 years

1 This section draws heavily on research by Kitty Stewart (2005b).

2 Given the rapid reduction in child poverty in the UK against this kind of standard since 1996/97 (see the lower part of table 10), this position may well now have improved, particularly by comparison with the US.

3 Stewart (2005b, fig. 14.13), using incomes before housing costs and the OECD equivalence scale. As we saw in table 2 above, after housing costs and using the McClements equivalence scale, 73 per cent of households with a chief wage earner out of work were counted as poor in Britain in 2001/02.

4 See Darton, Hirsch and Strelitz (2003), fig. 30.

5 See, for instance, Park et al. (2003) for results from the 2002 survey, including a description of the survey and how it is carried out in its appendices. For more detailed discussion of some of the results discussed in this section, see Hills (2001, 2004a).

6 It is also true that when respondents were asked in 2001 what proportion of children were poor, the median response was 25 per cent, also roughly in line with the official figures for child poverty against the 60 per cent of median income line (Taylor-Gooby and Hastie, 2002, appendix figure). However, responses to other questions of this kind, such as the proportion of social security going to unemployed people, were a long way from the mark, so some might temper the weight put on this finding.

7 By contrast, in the US, when people were asked to choose between two reasons for people living in need, 61 per cent blamed laziness or lack of willpower rather than society treating them unfairly (Hills, 2004a, p. 69, based on World Values Survey results).

8 John Hills acted as Secretary to the Inquiry Group.

9 See Sassi (2005) for a discussion.

10 See Hills (2004a), ch. 10, for a more detailed discussion, and the first report of the Pensions Commission, chaired by Adair Turner, published in October 2004, for a discussion of future prospects for pensions.

11 Wittenberg et al. (2004) show that there is a very large 'funnel of doubt' about future long term care costs, but the upside risk is considerable. On one scenario, if age-specific needs did not decline as life expectancy lengthens and care standards improve moderately, then with current demographic projections, total public and private long term care costs could rise from 1.4 per cent of GDP now to 3.4 per cent in 2051, with the state component rising from 0.9 to 2.3 per cent of GDP. If free personal care was extended from Scotland across the UK, in this scenario, the public costs would be another 0.75 per cent of GDP higher.

8 Poverty and progress for the next generation?

1 Hills and Stewart (2005), table 15.1.

2 Darton, Hirsch and Strelitz (2003), fig. 7.

3 Darton, Hirsch and Strelitz calculate that eradication of poverty within 20 years would require incomes of the poorest fifth to grow annually by 7 per cent per year, while other incomes grew by 2.5 per cent (2003, p. 15). They suggest that the aggregate 'poverty gap' to be closed is equivalent to about a fortieth of national income, or about a twentieth of expected gains from growth over the period. If this was achieved simply through income transfers, the

gross cost would be higher, of course, as it is hard to imagine successful policies that would affect only the poorest.

4 See the first report of the Pensions Commission, published in October 2004, for a discussion of the trade-offs between future pensioner living standards, retirement ages and levels of public and private pension contributions.

5 Alesina and Glaeser (2004) suggest that in the US racial and ethnic prejudices have been manipulated to support judgemental views about the poor. In Europe such views have been less judgemental, but the authors warn that the rapidly changing ethnic and social mix may change this in future.

References

Abbott, E. (1917) 'Charles Booth, 1840–1916', *Journal of Political Economy*, 25(2): 195–203.

Abel-Smith, B. and Townsend, P. (1965) *The poor and the poorest*, Occasional Papers in Social Administration 17, London: Bell.

Abrams, M. (1951) *Social surveys and social action*, London: Heinemann.

Acemoglu, D. (2003), 'Cross-country inequality trends', *Economic Journal*, 113(48): F21–49.

Alesina, A. and Glaeser, E. L. (2004) *Fighting poverty in the US and Europe: A world of difference*, Oxford: Oxford University Press.

Atkinson, A. B. (1969) *Poverty in Britain and the reform of social security*, Cambridge: Cambridge University Press.

Atkinson, A. B. (2000) 'Distribution of income and wealth', in A. H. Halsey and J. Webb (eds), *Twentieth-century British social trends*, Basingstoke: Macmillan.

Atkinson, A. B. and Micklewright, J. (1989) 'Turning the screw: Benefits for the unemployed 1979–1988', in A. Dilnot and I. Walker (eds), *The economics of social security*, Oxford: Oxford University Press.

Atkinson, A. B., Corlyon, J., Maynard, A. K., Sutherland, H. and Trinder, C. G. (1981) 'Poverty in York: A reanalysis of Rowntree's 1950 survey', *Bulletin of Economic Research*, 33: 59–71.

Baldwin, P. (1990) *The politics of social solidarity: Class bases of the European welfare state*, Cambridge: Cambridge University Press.

Baldwin, S. and Falkingham, J. (1994) *Social security and social change: New challenges to the Beveridge model*, Hemel Hempstead: Harvester Wheatsheaf.

Barclay, P. (chair) (1995) *Inquiry into income and wealth*, vol. 1: *Report of the inquiry group*, York: Joseph Rowntree Foundation.

Beckerman, W. and Clark, S. (1982) *Poverty and social security in Britain since 1961*, Oxford: Oxford University Press.

Behrendt, C. (2002) *At the margins of the welfare state: Social assistance and the alleviation of poverty in Germany, Sweden and the United Kingdom*, Aldershot: Ashgate.

Beveridge, W. (1942) *Social Insurance and Allied Services*, Cmd 6404, London: HMSO.

Blair, T. (1999) 'Beveridge revisited: A welfare state for the 21st century', in R. Walker (ed.), *Ending child poverty: Popular welfare for the 21st century*, Bristol: Policy Press.

Blaug, M. (1963) 'The myth of the old Poor Law and the making of the new', *Journal of Economic History*, 23: 151–84.

Booth, C. (1888) 'Condition and occupations of the people of East London and Hackney, 1887', *Journal of the Royal Statistical Society*, 51(2): 276–339.

Booth, C. (1891) 'Enumeration and classification of paupers, and state pensions for the aged', *Journal of the Royal Statistical Society*, 54(4): 600–43.

Booth, C. (1892–7) *Labour and life of the people in London*, London: Macmillan.

Bosanquet, H. (1903) 'The "poverty line"', *Charity Organisation Review*, 8(78): 321–5.

Bowley, A. L. and Burnett-Hurst, A. R. (1915) *Livelihood and poverty : A study in the economic conditions of working-class households in Northampton, Warrington, Stanley and Reading*, London: Bell and Sons.

Bowley, A. L. and Burnett-Hurst, A. R. (1920) *Economic conditions of working-class households in Bolton, 1914: A supplementary chapter to 'Livelihood and poverty'*, London: Bell and Sons.

Bowley, A. L. and Hogg, M. H. (1925) *Has poverty diminished? A sequel to 'Livelihood and poverty'*, London: King.

Bowpitt, G. (2000) 'Poverty and its early critics: The search for a value-free definition of the problem', in J. Bradshaw and R. Sainsbury (eds), *Getting the measure of poverty: The early legacy of Seebohm Rowntree*, Aldershot: Ashgate.

Bradshaw, J. (1993) *Budget Standards for the United Kingdom*, Aldershot: Avebury.

Bradshaw, J. and Finch, N. (2002) *A comparison of child benefit packages in 22 countries*, DWP Research Report 174, Leeds: Corporate Document Services.

Brewer, M., Duncan, A., Shephard, A. and Suárez, M. J. (2003) *Did Working Families' Tax Credit work? Analysing the impact of in-work support on labour supply and programme participation*, London: Inland Revenue and Institute for Fiscal Studies.

Brewer, M., Goodman, A., Myck, M., Shaw, J. and Shephard, A. (2004) *Poverty and inequality in Britain: 2004*, Commentary 96, London: Institute for Fiscal Studies.

Briggs, A. (1961) *Social thought and social action: A study of the work of Seebohm Rowntree, 1871–1954*, London: Longmans.

Brooks, B. (1986) 'Women and reproduction 1860–1919', in J. Lewis (ed.), *Labour and love: Women's experience of home and family 1950–1940*, Oxford: Blackwell.

Burchardt, T. (2005) 'Selective inclusion: Asylum seekers and other marginalised groups', in Hills and Stewart (2005).

Cole, D. and Utting, J. (1962) *The economic circumstances of old people,* Occasional Paper in Social Administration 4, London: Bell.

Congregational Union (1883) *The bitter cry of outcast London: An inquiry into the condition of the abject poor*, London: Congregational Union.

Darton, D., Hirsch, D. and Strelitz, J. (2003) *Tackling disadvantage: A 20-year enterprise*, York: Joseph Rowntree Foundation.

Desai, M. and Shah, A. (1988) 'An econometric approach to the measurement of poverty', *Oxford Economic Papers,* 40(3): 505–22.

DHSS (Department of Health and Social Security) (1988) *Low income families – 1985*, London: Government Statistical Service.

Donnison, D. (1982) *The politics of poverty*, Oxford: Martin Robertson.

DSS (Department of Social Security) (1999) *Opportunity for all: Tackling poverty and social exclusion*, London: DSS.

Dunkley, P. (1982) *The crisis of the old poor law in England 1700–1834: An interpretive essay*, New York: Garland.

DWP (Department for Work and Pensions) (2003a) *Households below average income 1994/95–2001/02*, Leeds: Corporate Document Services.

DWP (Department for Work and Pensions) (2003b) *Abstract of statistics for benefits, contributions and indices of prices and earnings*, 2002 edn, London: DWP.

DWP (Department for Work and Pensions) (2004) *Households below average income 1994/95–2002/03*, Leeds: Corporate Document Services.

Evans, M. (1998) 'Social security: Dismantling the pyramids?', in H. Glennerster and J. Hills (eds), *The state of welfare: The economics of social spending*, Oxford: Oxford University Press.

Evans, M. and Glennerster, H. (1993) 'Squaring the circle: The inconsistencies and constraints of Beveridge's plan', Welfare State Programme Discussion Paper 86, London: London School of Economics.

Fiegehen, G. C., Lansley, P. S. and Smith, A. D. (1977) *Poverty and Progress in Britain, 1953–73*, Cambridge: Cambridge University Press.

Ford, P. (1934) *Work and wealth in a modern port: A social survey of Southampton*, London: Allen and Unwin.

Fraser, D. (1973) *The evolution of the welfare state*, London: Macmillan.

Gallie, D. and Paugam, S. (2002) *Social precarity and social integration*, Brussels: European Commission (Employment and Social Affairs).

Gillie, A. (1996) 'The origin of the poverty line', *Economic History Review*, 49(4): 715–30.

Glendinning, C. (1992) *The costs of informal care: Looking inside the household*, London: SPRU/HMSO.

Glennerster, H. (2000) *British social policy since 1945*, Oxford: Blackwell.

Glennerster, H. (2002) 'United States poverty studies and poverty measurement: The past twenty-five years', *Social Service Review* (Mar.): 83–107.

Glennerster, H. and Evans, M. (1994) 'Beveridge and his assumptive worlds: The incompatibilities of a flawed design', in Hills, Ditch and Glennerster (1994).

Goodman, A. and Webb, S. (1994) *For richer, for poorer: The changing distribution of income in the United Kingdom, 1961–1991*, London: Institute for Fiscal Studies.

Gordon, D. and Townsend, P. (eds) (2000) *Breadline Europe: The measurement of poverty*, Bristol: Policy Press.

Gordon, D., Adelman, L., Ashworth, K., Bradshaw, J., Levitas, R., Middleton, S., Pantazis, C., Patsios, D., Payne, S., Townsend, P. and Williams, J. (2000) *Poverty and social exclusion in Britain*, York: Joseph Rowntree Foundation.

Gregg, P. and Wadsworth, J. (2001) 'Everything you ever wanted to ask about measuring worklessness and polarization at the household level but were afraid to ask', *Oxford Bulletin of Economics and Statistics*, 63 (special issue): 777–806.

Hagenaars, A. J. M. and Van Praag, B. M. S. (1985) 'A synthesis of poverty line definitions', *Review of Income and Wealth*, 31(2): 139–54.

Harkness, S. and Waldfogel, J. (2003) 'The family gap in pay: Evidence from seven industrialized countries', *Research in Labor Economics*, 22: 369–414.

Harris, J. (1972) *Unemployment and politics: A study of English social policy 1886–1914*, Oxford: Oxford University Press.

Harris, J. (1997) *William Beveridge: A biography* (1977), 2nd edn, Oxford: Oxford University Press.

Harris, J. (2002) 'From poor law to welfare state? A European perspective', in D. Winch and P. K. O'Brien (eds), *The political economy of British historical experience 1688–1914*, Oxford: Oxford University Press.

Hatton, T. J. and Bailey, R. E. (2000) 'Seebohm Rowntree and the post-war poverty puzzle', *Economic History Review*, 53(3): 517–43.

Hills, J. (1995) *Income and wealth*, vol. 2: *A survey of the evidence*, York: Joseph Rowntree Foundation.

Hills, J. (2001) 'Poverty and social security: What rights? Whose responsibilities?', in A. Park, J. Curtice, K. Thomson, L. Jarvis and C. Bromley (eds), *British social attitudes: The 18th report*, London: Sage.

Hills, J. (2004a) *Inequality and the state*, Oxford: Oxford University Press.

Hills, J. (2004b) 'Inclusion or insurance? National Insurance and the future of the contributory principle', *Journal of Social Policy*, 33: 347–72.

Hills, J. and Lelkes, O. (1999) 'Social security, selective universalism, and patchwork redistribution', in R. Jowell, J. Curtice, A. Park, and K. Thomson (eds), *British social attitudes: The 16th report*, Aldershot: Ashgate.

Hills, J. and Stewart, K. (eds) (2005), *A more equal society? New Labour, poverty, inequality and exclusion*, Bristol: Policy Press.

Hills, J., Ditch, J. and Glennerster H. (eds) (1994) *Beveridge and social security: An international retrospective*, Oxford: Oxford University Press.

HM Treasury (2003a) *Budget 2003: Building a Britain of economic strength and social justice*, HC500, London: TSO.

HM Treasury (2003b) *Pre-Budget report: The strength to take the long-term decisions for Britain*, Cm.6042, London: TSO.

HM Treasury (2004) *Child poverty review*, London: HM Treasury.

Horne, T. (1986) *Property rights and poverty: Political argument in Britain 1605–1834*, Exeter: Exeter University Press.

Innes, J. (1998) 'State, church and voluntarism in European welfare, 1690–1850', in H. Cunningham and J. Innes (eds), *Charity, philanthropy and reform*, Basingstoke: Macmillan.

Innes, J. (1999) 'The state and the poor: Eighteenth-century English poor relief in European context', in J. Brewer and E. Hellmuth (eds), *Rethinking Leviathan: The eighteenth-century state in Britain and Germany*, Oxford: Oxford University Press.

Innes, J. (2002) 'The distinctiveness of the English poor laws, 1750–1850', in D. Winch and P. K. O'Brien (eds), *The political economy of British historical experience 1688–1914*, Oxford: Oxford University Press.

Johnson, P. (1996) 'Risk, redistribution and social welfare in Britain from the Poor Law to Beveridge', in M. Daunton (ed.), *Charity, self interest and welfare in the English past*, London: Routledge.

Jones, D. C. (1934) *Social survey of Merseyside*, Liverpool: University Press of Liverpool.

Jowell, R., Curtice, J., Park, A., Thomson, K., Jarvis, L., Bromley, C. and Stratford, N. (eds) (2000) *British social attitudes: The 17th report*, London: Sage.

Kidd, A. (1999) *State, Society and the Poor in Nineteenth-Century England*, Basingstoke: Macmillan.

Kiernan, K., Land, H. and Lewis, J. (1998) *Lone motherhood in twentieth century Britain*, Oxford: Oxford University Press.

Kilpatrick, R. W. (1973) 'The income elasticity of the poverty line', *Review of Economics and Statistics*, 55(3): 327–32.

King, S. (2000) *Poverty and welfare in England, 1700–1850*, Manchester: Manchester University Press.

Lakin, C. (2003) 'The effects of taxes and benefits on household income, 2001/02002', *Economic Trends* (May): 1–47 (web version).

Lewis. J. and Piachaud, D. (1992) 'Women and poverty in the twentieth century', in C. Glendinning and J. Millar (eds), *Women and poverty in Britain*, Brighton: Wheatsheaf.

Lister, R. (2004) *Poverty*, Cambridge: Polity Press.

Llewellyn-Smith, H. (1930–5) *New survey of London life and labour*, London: King.

Lowe, R. (1999) *The welfare state in Britain since 1945*, Basingstoke: Macmillan.

Lupton, R. and Power, A. (2005) 'Disadvantaged by where you live? New Labour and neighbourhood renewal', in Hills and Stewart (2005).

Mack, J. and Lansley, S. (1985) *Poor Britain*, London: George Allen and Unwin.

Macnicol, J. (1980) *The movement for family allowances 1918–45*, London: Heinemann.

Macnicol, J. (1998) *The politics of retirement in Britain 1878–1948*, Cambridge: Cambridge University Press.

Mann, H. H. (1905) 'Life in an agricultural village in England', *Sociological Papers*, pp. 163–93.

Mayhew, H. (1861–2) *London labour and the London poor*, 4 vols, London.

McKnight, A. (2005) 'Employment: Tackling poverty through "work for those who can"', in Hills and Stewart (2005).

Michielse, H. C. M. (1990) 'Policing the poor: J. L. Vives and the sixteenth-century origins of modern social administration', *Social Service Review,* 64(1):1–21.

Millar, J. and Glendinning, C. (1987) 'Invisible women, invisible poverty', in C. Glendinning and J. Millar (eds) *Women and poverty in Britain*, Brighton: Wheatsheaf.

Minority Report, Royal Commission on the Poor Laws (1909) Minority Report of the Royal Commission on the Poor Laws and the Relief of Distress, London: HMSO.

Mitchell, D. (1991) *Income transfers in ten welfare states*, Aldershot: Avebury.

Owen, A. D. K. (1933) *A survey of the standard of living in Sheffield*, Survey Pamphlet 9, Sheffield: Social Survey Committee.

Oxley, H., Dang, T.-T. and Antolín, P. (1999) *Poverty dynamics in six OECD countries*, Paris: Organisation for Economic Co-operation and Development.

Pahl, J. (1989) *Money and marriage*, London: Macmillan.

Park, A., Curtice, J., Thomson, K., Jarvis, L. and Bromley, C. (eds) (2003) *British social attitudes: The 20th report*, London: Sage.

Parker, G. (1985) *With due care and attention*, London: Family Policy Studies Centre.

Pedersen, S. (1993) *Family, dependence and the origins of the welfare state in Britain and France 1914–1945*, Cambridge: Cambridge University Press.

Pember Reeves, M. S. (1914) 'Family life on a pound a week' (Fabian Tract No 162), London: Fabian Society. (The most accessible modern version is: S. Alexander (ed) (1988) *Women's source library vol. VII: Women's Fabian Tracts*, London: Routledge.)

Piachaud, D. (1981) 'Peter Townsend and the Holy Grail', *New Society*, 57 (10 Sept.): 419–21.

Piachaud, D. (1988) 'Poverty in Britain 1899 to 1983', *Journal of Social Policy*, 17(3): 335–49.

Rathbone, E. (1917) 'The remuneration of women's services', *Economic Journal*, 27 (Mar.): 55–68.

Rathbone, E. (1924) *The disinherited family*, London: Edward Arnold.

Rowntree, B. S. (1901) *Poverty: A study of town life*, London: Macmillan.

Rowntree, B. S. (1918) *The human needs of labour*, London: Nelson.

Rowntree, B. S (1937) *The human needs of labour*, new edn, revised and rewritten, London: Longmans Green.

Rowntree, B. S. (1941) *Poverty and progress: A second social survey of York*, London: Longmans.

Rowntree, B. S. (2001) *Poverty: A study of town life,* centennial edn, Bristol: Policy Press.

Rowntree, B. S. and Lavers, G. R. (1951) *Poverty and the welfare state: A third social survey of York dealing only with economic questions*, London: Longmans.

Royal Commission on the Poor Laws (1909) *Report*, London: HMSO.

Sassi, F. (2005) 'Tackling health inequalities', in Hills and Stewart (2005).

Sefton, T. (2002) *Recent changes in the distribution of the social wage*, CASE Paper 62, London: London School of Economics.

Sefton, T. and Sutherland, H. (2005) 'Inequality and poverty under New Labour', in Hills and Sutherland (2005).

Sen, A. (1983) 'Poor relatively speaking', *Oxford Economic Papers*, 35: 153–69.

Simey, T. S. and Simey, M. B. (1960) *Charles Booth: Social scientist*, Oxford: Oxford University Press.

Slack, P. (1988) *Poverty and policy in Tudor and Stuart England*, London: Longman.

Slack, P. (1990) *The English Poor Law, 1531–1782*, Basingstoke: Macmillan.

Smith, A. (1776) *An inquiry into the nature and causes of the wealth of nations*, London: Home University Library.

Stevenson, J. and Cook, C. (1979) *Society and politics during the Depression*, London: Quartet Books.

Stewart, K. (2005a) 'Towards an equal start? Addressing childhood poverty and deprivation', in Hills and Stewart (2005).

Stewart, K. (2005b) 'Changes in poverty and inequality in the UK in international context', in Hills and Stewart (2005).

Taylor, R. M. (1938) *A social survey of Plymouth: Second report*, London: P. S. King and Son.

Taylor-Gooby, P. and Hastie, C. (2002) 'Support for state spending: Has New Labour got it right?', in A. Park, J. Curtice, K. Thomson, L. Jarvis and C. Bromley (eds), *British social attitudes: The 19th report*, London: Sage.

Thatcher, A. R. (1968) 'The distribution of earnings of employees in Great Britain', *Journal of the Royal Statistical Society*, series A, 131(2): 133–70.

Timmins, N. (1995) *The five giants: A biography of the welfare state*, London: HarperCollins.

Tout, H. (1938) *The standard of living in Bristol*, Bristol: Arrowsmith.

Townsend, P. (1954) 'Measuring poverty', *British Journal of Sociology*, 5(2): 130–7.

Townsend, P. (1962) 'The meaning of poverty', *British Journal of Sociology*, 13(3): 210–27.

Townsend, P. (1979) *Poverty in the United Kingdom: A survey of household resources and standards of living*, Harmondsworth: Penguin.

UNICEF (United Nations Children's Fund) (2000) *A league table of child poverty in rich nations*, Innocenti Report Card 1, Florence: Innocenti Research Centre.

Van Reenen, J. (2004) 'Active labor market policies and the British New Deal for unemployed youth in context', in R. Blundell, D. Card and R. Freeman (eds), *Seeking a premier league economy*, Chicago: University of Chicago Press.

Veit-Wilson, J. (1986) 'Paradigms of poverty: A rehabilitation of B. S. Rowntree', *Journal of Social Policy*, 15(1): 69–99.

Veit-Wilson, J. (1994) 'Condemned to deprivation? Beveridge's responsibility for the invisibility of poverty', in Hills, Ditch and Glennerster (1994).

Wardley, P. and Woollard, M. (1994) 'Retrieving the past: A reclamation and reconstruction of the social survey of Bristol, 1937', *History and Computing*, 6(2): 85–105

Webb, J. (2002) 'Always with us? The evolution of poverty in Britain, 1886–2002', D.Phil. thesis, University of Oxford, Oxford.

Webb, B. and Webb, S. (1929) *English local government: English Poor Law history,* London: Longmans

Wedderburn, D. (1962) 'Poverty in Britain today: The evidence', *Sociological Review* 10(3): 257–82.

Whiteside, N. (1983) 'Private agencies for public purposes: Some perspectives on policy making in health insurance between the wars', *Journal of Social Policy,* 12, P2: 165–94.

Wittenberg, R., Comas-Herrara, A., Pickard, L. and Hancock, R. (2004) *Future demand for long-term care in the UK: A summary of projections of long-term care finance for older people to 2051,* York: Joseph Rowntree Foundation.